I Have Given You Everything

Anna McAllister

Cover designed by Mark McAllister, Markit Publishing
Printed in the United Kingdom by UK Print

Contents

Preface

"God is able to take your life with all of the heartache, all of the pain, all of the regret and all of the missed opportunities and use you for His Glory"
Charles R. Swindoll.

I love to tell stories. Words, when carefully put together, can express to a blind person a vision that you and I take for granted. Words constructed in the right manner can bring colour to the description of a dull and boring rainy day. But ultimately, when spoken or written with conviction, words used for the Glory of God can breathe life into the most desperate of situations. There is a line in a song that I love that says, 'you caught my soul when I was struggling to breathe'. It speaks so powerfully of my reason for writing this book. I struggled for so long with depression that I thought it was normal. One day in the midst of this nightmare, I believe that God stopped me in my tracks and made sure that the impact of seizing my attention at that moment would change my life forever.

I live in a community where depression and suicide have become commonplace. Friends have lost husbands and sons. Even my kids have experienced the tragedy of losing school friends as teenagers who believed that the only solution to their situation was suicide. This trend is not exclusive to my part of the country either. There are websites that are devoted to helping those who are tormented, ready to leave this mortal plain. What on earth is this world coming to when our family and friends who need help have such easy access to some of the most destructive advice imaginable? I am not judging, for I was sadly one of the many. I say *was* because I know now that there is a way out of this darkness - His name is Jesus. My reason for sharing this story is to destroy the myth that depression is normality for some and not others. I don't believe that it has to be a normality for anyone. I am restored back to health after one counselling session with God, and this is my account of what happened that night.

My mum always said I could write a book, but I always joked that my wayward past might mean that I inadvertently referred to characters who would recognize themselves and sue, in which case there wouldn't be any point as they are the most interesting stories. In all seriousness, though, I do love to tell stories, but the content of those stories has changed over the years and now my aim is to bring glory to God with the words He has given me. I have friends who have listened to my stories time and time again and I thank you all for your patience as I will probably tell them again. But I am playing it safe and talking only about me, so you lovely people who panicked when they realised I had written a book can relax for this one.

I would like to thank the Reading Circle (yes that is what I am going to call you from now on) - Brenda, Helen, Maggie and Mandy - who painstakingly read and corrected my grammar and spelling so that it all made sense to everyone else. You gave me confidence throughout this whole process, and I could not have put this together without you. Thanks also to Anna and Lance,who have been friends and companions to both myself and my husband Mark, throughout this journey. Without your constant encouragement and input during the rewrites of each chapter, this book would never have been finished. To Lewis who gave up his time to counsel and encourage me never to give up, you went above and beyond the call of duty and I will be forever grateful for your faithfulness. Finally, to my family: kids, even though I embarrass you at times, please remember that job is not exclusive to your father yelling and screaming on sports day when you were at school. Just be thankful this story is about me and I am not letting out all your secrets. I love you all and, I am proud of each one of you. Mark, you are my gift from God. Without you encouraging me to study and fulfil my dreams, I would still be cooking stew in the school canteen. You have supported me in every ridiculous and impulsive, hair-brained idea that I have ever come up with and you have never let me down. Maybe it is you who is the crazy one, not me.

So here we go, if God can use a donkey to speak in Numbers 22, then He can use me. My prayer is that you pass this message of hope onto others that they will also find freedom through Christ our Saviour.

Chapter 1
Living Like a Lunatic

"Oh what a tangled web we weave, when first
we practise to deceive"
Sir Walter Scott.

As I looked through the window of my house that was just waking up to a beautiful Saturday morning, I realised that I had been sitting in the driver's seat of my car for two hours. It was 10.30 am and I had no idea where the time had gone or why I was still sitting there in my car. I had been up since 6.00 am, cooking bacon and sausages for the men's meeting in the church, and after serving the breakfast I had left them to it and drove home about 8.30. Two full hours had gone by and I just sat there in my driveway, staring through the windows of my family home. As I watched everyone whom I loved wake up and start their day, I just did not want to leave the car to join them. They made breakfast and watched Saturday morning TV, Mark, my husband picked up their dishes and washed them at the sink in the kitchen that had made me want this house so badly a few years before when we bought it. Now I don't even want to go in, I found no joy in it anymore, so I watched. The first suicidal thought was that they would be just fine without me. It was subtle, you couldn't even connect it as a suicidal thought at first. 'They will be fine without me' could mean a divorce which was on the cards anyway, it didn't mean I was about to go into the garage and throw a rope up. It was just a thought. Everyone looked so happy and I was so unhappy. It felt like it all turned to chaos whenever I would walk through the door, so the easiest thing would be not to go in. It seemed logical to me - I just would not go in ever again. But I wasn't making any moves to drive away either, I had no idea what I was going to do next, I was just sitting there.

Just then, Mark noticed me sitting in the car and came out and asked, 'What are you doing sitting out here, are you not coming in?' I didn't know, I had no answers, I really didn't know anything anymore. It just made sense not to go in. By this stage the kids had started to notice and Mark had to go in and tell them that I had forgotten something and needed to go back to the shops. He told me to move over to the passenger seat and he began to drive. Our marriage had been on the rocks for a long time. Mark had been trying to hide my strange behaviour from everyone and he was at the end of his tether. The conversation began, as many had, 'this has to stop, it can't go on, the kids are noticing, you're unpredictable, I never know what you are going to say or do next.......' I can't really remember the rest, but as he drove and talked I knew that they would be much better off without me.

He stopped at a corner shop where we got chocolate always a pick me up when you are miserable and he drove to Browns Bay where we sat in silence. I put the window down and listened to the sound of the waves. I love the sound of the sea, it is so peaceful. The sea seemed to drown out the voices and the confusion that never left my head. So, we sat there while my ears filled with the roar of the waves as they rolled in.

As the swells broke on the shore, my anxiety levels began to subside and this beautiful sound of nature filled the awkward silence between us. Here we were two people who no longer knew each other, who no longer wanted to be in each other's company and who were trapped in a world of misery that revolved around my depression.

The next thing I remember was waking up. Mark had his arm around me and for a split second I felt normal. I always felt safe when Mark put his arm around me. I think I even remember smiling at that moment, but it didn't last. The voices came flooding back in an instant and I remembered the rows and the screaming and the yelling and the bitterness. The reality of what my life had become jolted me back so quickly that I sat up straight asking how long I had been asleep. You should not have let me sleep so long, attacking him, accusing him. Mark quickly came back to reality too; 'you needed the sleep', he said in a hostile way. Mark knew not to let his guard down or I would quickly use the opportunity to spew out all the irritation and anger I was feeling. I was caught unawares, falling asleep the way I had that day, but sleep was not something I had the luxury of enjoying lately and after three hours' sleeping in the car I felt rested, a bit calmer and not so aggressive. 'You're right!' was all I remember saying as I cried and promised to try to get it all under control again. However, this was not the first time nor the last that

Mark would hear these empty words. I might have been saying the right thing, but we both knew I was 'out to lunch' most of the time on the pills I had come to depend on, so the many remorseful words that I spoke sank into the abyss of promises that now existed. The gap had become immense between us and my words no longer held any value in this marriage.

Feeling rested, the urge to jump off this rollercoaster had subsided for a while, so we headed home where I found comfort in a movie and a large bag of crisps. As long as there was noise, any kind of noise - a radio or TV running in the background - drowning out the voices, I could cope. But when left in silence, the madness was unbearable. I couldn't sleep, I couldn't think and there were so many voices in my head it made me want to scream. So I had learned to mask it and disguise it with a louder noise, a blaring TV or radio meant I could ignore the commotion during the day. After this event in Browns Bay I thought I had discovered the solution to help me sleep at night. I wore headphones in bed and a YouTube video of the sea, which played all night, helped me sleep like a baby for a while. Another coping mechanism to drown out the deranged thoughts of this crazy, manic depressive. I could survive a bit longer.

I had suffered from depression once before. The cause had been a bad break up with my boyfriend at the age of 20 which had plunged me into the depths of despair. It lasted about six months and I found myself doing crazy things then too, like housework at four in the morning or walking the streets with the two girls in the pram in the early hours and talking to myself. I thought it was just a glitch in the past and of course I could blame it on the ex. Never would I have dreamed that I would find myself in such a dark place again. But here I was three years into a bout of depression that had no notion of shifting, and no anti-depressant or sleeping pill was giving me the peace that I so desperately needed.

I had two beautiful daughters and two handsome sons, a husband who loved me and worshipped the ground I walked on (or at least he did when this all started). I had a lovely home, a family who loved me and a pretty good life, so what had I to be depressed about? I was a Christian with a very supportive and loving church family and friends whom I still hold in high regard today as they stuck with me throughout this time. So what was my problem?

I had been diagnosed by my GP as a *Manic Depressive* - a label that would stick as a permanent reminder for the rest of my life. A cocktail of Prozac and Temazepam were my goto solutions every day, and I realised that the only way that anyone could get away from this curse was for me not to exist. I couldn't do life this way for the next forty years, but, if I am honest, I really didn't have the courage to end it all.

I thought I had found a solution to that problem too. One night, in an hysterical rant I asked Mark to do it. Now, I would not recommend that you ask the man whom you have been torturing with your mood swings and madness for the past three years to help you kill yourself; he might be tempted. But the truth is I did, more than once. I remember pleading with him to put something in my food and leave the bottle beside my bed and no one would ever know. My doctor would say that I was depressed, my friends would say that they had noticed a difference in me and no-one would ever blame the poor husband who had had so much to put up with. It would obviously be suicide, I would be put out of my misery, everyone could carry on and no one would ever know it had been Mark. I would become a distant memory and it wouldn't take long for everything to settle down, especially since I was making everyone so unhappy now. Surely they would be relieved to be rid of such a massive burden of looking after the family screwball. It made sense to me that he should help me.

I would like to point out that Mark was the only one who knew just how bad this whole situation had become. I had sworn him to secrecy. I am also very glad that the madness was not contagious. If Mark had taken me up on my request, I would not be here to tell the tale. He was, however, in a terrible position. I was devious enough to understand that, if I told my doctor that I was suicidal, I might do a wee stint in the local nuthouse. Also, if I revealed all to my pastor who was counselling me at the time, then I might look like someone who was not good enough to be in his church or even be called a Christian (this was my paranoid perception, you understand, not his). Pride, or keeping up appearances, kept me from ever getting the help that I really needed, so I struggled on, making Mark suffer with me, forcing him to live a lie. He made excuses for me and all for the sake of preserving my dignity or what was left of it. There should have been a get-out clause in our wedding vows, instead of 'till death do us part', we should have had 'until the craziness sets in'. Outside the walls of my house I could put on a hell of a show, but inside everything was so weird that it is hard to explain even today.

I did have one friend whom I worked with who could see right through the façade that I had created. Christine spent many mornings talking me down off the ledge just so that we could get a day's work done. Although I don't think that even she realised just how often I played with the idea of taking my own life, if at all. Choosing my words carefully when I spoke, and avoiding situations that I would not be able to control or manipulate, meant that I spent a lot of time making up excuses and deceiving the people around me.

Paranoia ruled and I believed if I could stay one step ahead of those people who were out to get me then I would not be discovered as the crazy lunatic that I had become. One day, after I had spent two hours in what I can only call a counselling session from hell with the Pastor, I got into my car. You have no idea how hard it is to try to say the right things and pretend you understand and are making progress for two hours, especially when the man counselling you is well trained and has probably seen it all before. My pastor is a mighty man of God who was genuinely trying to help me and, looking back, he must have had the patience of a saint to continue counselling me. Totally fed up with the lack of progress and exhausted by the dance we had just done, I was ready to give up. The voices had gotten so loud that my radio wasn't drowning them out. I felt like a bomb had gone off in my head and the screaming and shouting and pain of the tormenting thoughts were unbearable. My head was pounding and I'd had enough. I made the decision to go home and take all of the sleeping pills that I had, just so that it would all be over. I started the car and headed home - I finally had the way out.

Almost immediately, a small voice spoke. It didn't come from inside my head, nor was it screaming to be heard, but it impacted me so much that I will never forget the three words that changed my life: 'KNOW YOUR ENEMY.' I knew that this was the voice of God because instantly the battle of the voices began. 'Why would God speak to you?'

KNOW YOUR ENEMY!

'God wouldn't want to speak to you not now after all this time!'

'KNOW YOUR ENEMY!'

'It would be so easy; just take the pills'

'KNOW YOUR ENEMY!'

'What is this 'know your enemy' about? You are just imagining things.'

This continued until I got home, and each time the thoughts came, God's voice said, 'KNOW YOUR ENEMY!' By the time I had pulled into my driveway I knew that I needed to know more. I felt like someone had taken a tiny spark and placed it inside me - a glimmer of hope that would not - dare I say, could not, be extinguished by the voices in my head. There was no doubt in my mind that this was God and I was excited. What I sensed for the first time in a very long time was the Holy Spirit stir up life and hope in me. I needed to continue this conversation and so I rushed into the house that I had previously dreaded entering. Although I didn't know it yet, this night would change my life and my family's life forever.

Living Like a Lunatic

Chapter 2
Know Your Enemy

"If you know your enemy and know yourself,
you need not fear the results of a hundred battles."
Sun Tzu

'Know Your Enemy' is a simple phrase that I have heard used many times but I had no idea where it came from or even who had said it. When I walked into my house that night, Mark had started dinner and the kids were watching TV. I was on a mission to hold on to the glimmer of hope that I had experienced twenty minutes beforehand. I told Mark what had happened and that I had to find out what 'know your enemy' meant. He googled it, as we all do these days, and there it was, 'if you know your enemy and know yourself, you need not fear the results of a hundred battles.' It was accredited to a Chinese military specialist, Sun Tzu, who is named as the author of The Art of War. The book itself was only properly translated into English in the twentieth century, but these words of wisdom had been around since 500 BC. I don't think I had ever heard the full quote until that day, but what followed led me to understand that, in order to live this life with a clear mind and for Gods' purpose, I must 'know my enemy'. Before the night was out, I would understand much more than a philosophical phrase found on google, I would have the key that unlocked the tormented mind that I had been living with and I would understand true peace.

So I left Mark to finish dinner and I went into my bedroom, got out my Bible, a notebook, some post-it notes and a pen. I sat down in the middle of my bed and simply said, 'God show me'. I opened my Bible, but where should I start? The strange thing is, looking back now, I was not conscious of the silence I was sitting in. The voices that had totally consumed me for so long were not drowning out my sanity, and the calm that was in that room was unexplainable. During my manic rants to God that I called prayer, I would ask, 'Why me? Why are you allowing me to have such a miserable life?' Now I asked God a different question calmly and confidently; in the stillness of my bedroom I asked, 'God, who is my enemy?'

John 10:10 was the first scripture that came to mind and so I turned to it,

> 'The thief comes only to steal and kill and destroy. I came that they may have life and have it abundantly.' (ESV)

Surely this isn't it, God! I know this scripture, I know the thief is my enemy, but the doctors say I am a manic depressive. I have a mental illness and my serotonin levels are low. The medication did work sometimes, I think! I have a diagnosis. Is it possible that all this time I was being deceived by a thief so that I couldn't function as a normal human being? Isn't that a bit extreme? I believe in the supernatural power of God. I also believe in miracles of Jesus and I believe that they happen today. In fact, I have seen amazing miracles with my own eyes when people were healed from illnesses that doctors couldn't explain. I have also seen people freed from all kinds of addictions instantly as the Holy Spirit moves in their lives. So, when I read about the supernatural and the power of God, I have no problems believing in the mighty things that God can do. So, if I believe in the supernatural, then it makes perfect sense that the fight that I had been engaged in for my sanity had actually been a deception from a thief, who wanted me to believe that I was mentally ill.

Let's take time to look at this logically. Did I not say previously that I had nothing to be depressed about and that, if truth be told, I had a lovely life with my family and extended Christian family? The joy of this truth alone had been stolen many years previously as I started to slip into depression with the lie that they would be better off without me. My marriage had almost been damaged beyond repair during these past few years, destroyed by hurtful, devastating words that had been said and could not be taken back. Once those petty arguments start and are in full flow, you say more than you should; and angry rants get so abusive and destructive that there is no way that you can pretend they hadn't happened. So, the story so far: my joy has been stolen, my marriage has been destroyed and my will to live was long gone. Score: 3-0 to the thief.

> *I came that they would have life more abundantly*

So, now that I knew what the enemy could do and how he had clearly influenced me, I began to look at what form he took. You see, I find that the red devil, with the horns, the pointy tail and the pitch fork, has become such a ridiculous image of Satan that we have been anaesthetized to just how malevolent he really is. I found a description of him in Ephesian 6:12.

> 'For we wrestle not against flesh and blood, but against principalities, against powers, against the rulers of the darkness of this world, against spiritual wickedness in high places.'
> (KJV)

There is nothing as obvious as a red devil here when the Bible describes the ruler of darkness. You see, I had been living in this world that Paul describes in his letter to the Ephesians for a few years at this point. Although I had read this scripture many times, isn't it amazing that I never really understood that I was living with Satan's influence. The amplified version gives me a fuller description; and when I read it I knew that this certainly spoke of the circumstances that I was facing.

We are deceived by the world view of the devil

'For our struggle is not against flesh and blood [contending only with physical opponents], but against the rulers, against the powers, against the world forces of this [present] darkness, against the spiritual forces of wickedness in the heavenly (supernatural) places.'
(Ephesians 6:12 AMP)

I was fighting all right in everyday life. I was fighting Mark and the kids, my Pastor and even my doctor; every opportunity to attack or defend, I took it. I hadn't picked the wrong battle I was fighting every battle, both real and imaginary, and I thought everyone was my enemy. I had been convinced that the depression I suffered was a physical illness and that, if my brain would just produce the right chemicals to keep me from slipping into dark, vicious angry moods, then I would be ok. I really had thought that the flesh and blood was my enemy, a stupid body that didn't function right. But this small verse revealed to me that the enemy I battled every day was a darkness, a spiritual force that had totally consumed me. I felt like a light bulb had suddenly gone on in this very dark world of mine and I wanted to see more of what God had to show me. This spiritual dynamic that I had lived in wasn't just exclusive to me; nor was depression a modern affliction I even found cases in the Old Testament.

I remember thinking that I had heard something about Elijah lying down somewhere and wanting to give up. So I looked for that story next: 1 Kings 19:1-10.

'But he himself went a day's journey into the wilderness and came and sat down under a broom tree. And he asked that he might die, saying, "It is enough; now, O LORD, take away my life, for I am no better than my fathers.'
(1Kings 19:4 ESV)

Oh my goodness, was Elijah suicidal? This great prophet, this mighty man of God, is it really possible for someone like him to be depressed? Elijah had just called down fire from heaven and shown the worshipers of Baal who the one true God was and they had turned to God - a great victory in my book. When Jezebel threatened him he ran away; this great man of faith ran and hid under a tree in the desert and asked God to take him. Maybe it was just a bad day or a low day - and I have had many of those. But no, this wasn't a bad day, doubt and fear had crept up on him and consumed him. He even says, 'it is enough'. How many times had I said that in the past few years, the straw that broke the camel's back. Like Elijah, I had reached that moment in chapter one. The physical and emotional exhaustion had weakened my desire to continue that day in my driveway, and it was the same here when we read about Elijah. Under that tree he needed sleep and food and water enough to sustain him for the journey ahead, we are told. I was beginning to grasp that this moment in time would be the same for me.

In my bedroom that night my thirst and hunger were being satisfied by Mark who was bringing me food and keeping my tea-cup topped up while I studied. However, my rest I found in God's word. I knew that all of my questions would be answered just by reading and talking to God. I was reading about others who had faced these same struggles and battles that I had. Great men of God, like Elijah, who the enemy had deceived into a place of total chaos of the mind, where he had forgotten that the God he served was more than capable of dealing with the Jezebels of this world.

'A person's spirit sustains him through sickness– but who can bear a crushed spirit?'
(Proverbs 18:14 NET)

The enemy is devious and if he can break the spirit of a person, causing chaos and confusion, the person under this influence would have no concept of serenity. Here I was living with very little sleep and I was physically and emotionally exhausted. I had isolated myself from all support by hiding how I really felt from those who were trying to help me. I had accepted that I was ill, but I now understood that the enemy had used my weakened state to break my spirit. How underhanded was this? I was becoming increasingly aware that I was not in a fair fight and it was never going to be a fair fight. But, with every passing moment in my bedroom that night the odds were getting better. God had sought out Elijah as he hid under the tree and then 40 days later in the cave; and God was doing the same for me. The loneliness lie was being exposed and I knew beyond all doubt that I was never going to feel alone again. The enemy had tried and succeeded in breaking my spirit - that is, until now.

There were other stories I remembered, other people that God had rescued from the clutches of the enemy's lies. That is the sad truth of this horrible condition which we casually call depression. It is not a new tactic of the enemy, it had been used for thousands of years, and people who suffer from it are being fooled into believing that they are the only ones. The shame and embarrassment of not being the 'full shilling', as they say where I come from, allows this guilty secret to stay hidden under the shadow of humiliation. However, there were great men of God, like Jonah and Elijah, who had walked where I had walked and lived as I had lived. They were still privy to the promises of God and were still part of His plan and purposes.

There are many more like this and, although the word 'depression' is not used in the Bible, I recognised the darkness and the moods that were being described in the lives of these men. It was almost as though the title 'depression' was hiding the truth behind the depth of this affliction. The intensity of the torment endured by someone living with depression has been diminished over time through a dumbing-down of the symptoms. We as a society think that if someone suffers from depression that all they have to do is pull themselves together. A positive mental attitude is all that is needed to turn that frown upside down. Unfortunately, that is not an option for someone who has been oppressed by this disorder for so long. I was beginning to see this spiritual dynamic for what it really was a thief to whom I had given permission to enter my life and who I entertained every day because I didn't know his identity.

Depression is not a modern affliction

I used the word 'disorder' to describe depression above and that really is an appropriate description. My mind was not in order there was total mayhem and chaos and as I read about the other people of God who had experienced this, I understood that confusion had been a greater tool than I had imagined. If I couldn't think straight, then my grip on reality was being impaired. What I thought was real, was not; and what was real seemed like an illusion. If you remember, in chapter one when I woke up after sleeping in the car and Mark had his arm around me,

31

I said that I remembered smiling for a moment and then reality set in. I was living in a world that was back to front. The deception was that, when Mark put his arm around me, the enemy had decieved me into believing that safety and security was a thing of the past. Too much had been said, too much water had flowed under the bridge, it wasn't possible for us to reconcile our differences, it could never be how it used to be...... Lies! Lies! Lies!

The weapons of the enemy were easy to spot when you knew what to look for. The enemy was a cheat and a liar, a thief and a murderer, a destructive force that had taken my sanity, my peace and my joy. All of these things he did to stop me from functioning like a normal human being, so that he could hold me back from the success of a contented life, both with my family and as a fully effective servant in God's kingdom. Worse still, my enemy is the enemy of the world, and everyone who is suffering from depression is in the same boat as me. Don't think that, because someone is not a Christian they are not going to be tormented by this evil and their depression is different from mine. The enemy will deceive everyone, not just the Christians. Satan isn't limited to believers only, his objective is to 'kill, steal and destroy' without partiality. So, if he can conquer the lives of people before they ever understand that they have a Saviour in Jesus, then he is gaining ground. You have heard the saying that 'the best defence is offence'. The devil isn't going to wait until you become a Christian to affect your life, he is gaining territory in this battle at every opportunity. You are not exempt just because you think you don't believe in God. Satan doesn't care if you are a believer or non-believer, his remit is to target everyone. The Bible says,

> *'Be sober-minded; be watchful. Your adversary the devil prowls around like a roaring lion, seeking someone to devour.'*
> *(1Peter 5:8 ESV)*

The devil isn't an adversary of Christians only, he is the adversary of the world, and there are no opt-out clauses when he is seeking someone, anyone, to devour. So, it really doesn't matter what or who you believe in, you are not immune from the destructive nature of this enemy. Unbelievers should not be under the illusion that, because they sit on the fence in their opinions as to whether God exists or not, the devil has no quarrel with them. He has no problems engaging with anyone in battle and has no tolerance for preferences or beliefs. He will take you out before you even realise that you are in a battle.

Don't we see these strategies in the games we play? Board games, sports, video games have the ultimate aim of victory over the opponent. Gain as much ground as you can before the challenger can outwit or outsmart you into a position of surrender or defeat.

It is the same in this battle that I was engaged in for my sanity. In this battle the enemy used a strong offensive action (depression) to preoccupy the opposition (me) and ultimately hinder my ability to mount a counterattack giving him a strategic advantage over me. No wonder Paul says in his letter to the Ephesians,

> *'Put on the whole armour of God, that you may be able to stand against the schemes of the devil.'*
> *(Ephesians 6:11 ESV)*

I had forgotten I even had armour. God had shown me who my enemy was, clearly and precisely in His word, we are warned about him and, in my presumption that I had understood the scriptures and stories that I had grown up with, I hadn't gone to them to look for the prescription for my illness. I had just gone to the doctor who was, I must say, very supportive; but she did not have the solution, just the man made potions that would manage the symptoms.

Your adversary the devil prowls around like a roaring lion

Now, armed with the knowledge of who my enemy was, the next stage in my quest to find sanity and retain my hope in God, was to understand who I was.

The enemy had succeeded in convincing me that I was a lunatic who was an embarrassment to my family and also to God, that I was defective in some way, but God was about to blow that subterfuge right out of the water, as you will see in the next chapter. I now know who you are, enemy, and things are about to change big time.

Chapter 3
Know Yourself

'But for all who did receive and trust in Him,
He gave them the right to be reborn as
children of God'
(John 1:12 The Voice)

As I was beginning to understand the lengths and breadths that the enemy would go to, I knew there was more to this battle than just knowing the enemy. There was a bit more to the quote that Mark and I had found on the internet, which was:

"If you know the enemy and know yourself, you need not fear the result of a hundred battles. If you know yourself but not the enemy, for every victory gained you will also suffer a defeat." SunTzu

I had lived in complete defeat because I did not know my enemy, and I wanted to live in total victory now that I was aware that that was an option for someone like me. However, I had no idea who I was any more. I thought I was supposed to be a wife and mother, but I wasn't really very good at that. Considering the mistakes I had made over the years, it certainly wasn't a natural talent of mine. I wasn't really a good Christian either, taking into account that I was supposed to have Jesus living in me. There wasn't much space in me for anyone to live, bearing in mind how the enemy had been partying with my sanity for years. So who was I? If I wanted to even the odds in this battle, I needed to know who I was too. The score was now 3-1 and I was clawing back some ground. For the first time in a long time, I was feeling optimistic; but I needed God to reveal more about how to win this battle.

Now I knew who Satan said I was because I had been listening to those voices for so long that I believed them as truth. Terrible mother, incompetent wife, disappointing daughter all of these titles I had lived with because I believed I deserved them based on some seriously stupid choices that I had made. (By the way these were all titles I had given myself, just in case you think I have cruel friends and family.) There were parts of my life that I really wanted to keep from God. You know we are talking about the creator of the universe, who in Genesis saw that His creation was good. Surely He must have been looking at what He created in me and wondered what went wrong.

At this point I could have really gone down a road that would normally have taken me a long time to come back from. But, instead of listening to the slanderer and liar that accuses, God's voice again spoke to me, 'Who are you?' My reply came instantly and without hesitation, 'I am a child of God'. Alone that night in my bedroom, when these words came out of my mouth, I almost looked around to see who had spoken. I don't think I had ever said this out loud before to describe myself; if I had, it had been so long ago that I had forgotten. I had certainly heard this phrase on thousands of occasions, but, mixed up somewhere with the lies, I believed that it was meant for everyone else in the Christian world except me. The enemy had intended to keep me isolated from

God and, because I had only listened to him, that is exactly what had happened I had been isolated.

'The one who lives alone is self-indulgent,
showing contempt for all who have
sound judgment.'
(Proverbs 18:1 NRS)

Isolation had caused loneliness and, as I thought no-one had any idea what it was like living with depression, I felt alone. The loneliness had produced a fear that I would have to spend the rest of my life trapped in this world of insanity. This fear caused bitterness to rise up as I watched all the normal people enjoy their marriages and perfect family lives. The most annoying twist of all was watching the flawless Christians achieving their new and improved life through Jesus as they were saved and forgiven and their sins forgotten. In an instant, as I spoke these words about me, there was a real confidence that I AM a child of God. It is funny how I knew that this statement was true, even though I had never attributed it to myself. There were many times that I had disputed this fact. Have you ever argued that what you read about in God's word doesn't apply to you? No! Just me then. I had lived under the suggestion that, because of my past, I wasn't worthy to be called a 'child of God', that I was a fake and a fraud in the Christian world because I suffered from depression. I had made many mistakes, and the biggest fear of all was that I might eventually be found out. This added to the constant paranoia that had engulfed my life, and I argued with God about what applied to me and what didn't.

'If we confess our sins, he is faithful and just
to forgive us our sins and to cleanse us
from all unrighteousness.'
(1 John 1:9 ESV)

I did not believe that this verse applied to me either, as I saw myself as dark and twisted, not clean and righteous. I am saved, I know that, I just don't remember when I started to doubt my salvation. However, what God was asking me here wasn't what I thought about myself; God wanted me to remember how He saw me something that in the confusion and chaos, I had not considered for a long time. I knew how I saw myself, I knew how some exes saw me, and I even thought I knew how my husband and children saw me, and that's where the fiction takes hold. I can read people's minds, you know. I believe that the word to describe this superpower is discernment. By the way, there are words and phrases that Christians use that are unfamilar to those outside Christian circles. There are also clichés that do not make sense and are just thrown out there for Christian special effect in a conversation. This is called Christianese. I hear clichés and statements used in Christian circles and run with it, not truely understanding their meaning;

and 'using the gift of discernment' was something I didn't really understand. Am I the only one who has done this? Anyway, this is how it worked for me: if Mark said he loved me, I heard the words but I knew what he really meant, I could see it in his eyes or in the look that I thought he gave me just as he walked past. I know what you are thinking 'oh that poor man' and I agree he put up with a lot. I didn't aim all of my paranoia at him, just most of it. Most of the people I know were accused during this period of madness. I would see the looks people would give me in church some tolerated me, others knew what I was, and those who didn't must be new and haven't realised yet that I am the crazy one. Paranoia was a great weapon that the enemy used against me for a few years. Now I have so many ridiculous anecdotes that I could put on my own stage show - The Paranoid Delusions of a Middle-aged Nutcase! Maybe that should be my next book.

"He is faithful and just to forgive our sins"

I digress. Back to the original question, 'who does God say that I am?' I started to remember phrases and began to look for them in my Bible and put post-it notes in the verses I found so that I wouldn't forget.

'Therefore, if anyone is in Christ, he is a new creation. The old has passed away; behold, the new has come.'
(2 Corinthians 5:17 ESV)

41

I am a new creation, the old me hadn't passed away, at least that is what I thought, but only because I held on to it. I had wanted God's forgiveness and I had wanted the slate wiped clean, but I had guessed that God's forgiveness was partial and dished out based on the enormity of the sin. Wrong! Another one of the enemy's lies. There are no conditions around this verse in Corinthians, there are no limits to the forgiveness of God. When the Word says that the old has gone and the new has come, that's exactly what it means. I had truly repented all of those years ago and there was no need for a resurrection of the past every time I wanted to indulge in a pity party. I am in Christ and I am a new creation, the old me has passed away and for this reason the new has come.

I am a child of God

'*For you did not receive the spirit of slavery to fall back into fear, but you have received the Spirit of adoption as sons, by whom we cry, "Abba! Father!"'*
(Romans 8:15 ESV)

Originally when I read the verse above, I was focused on the words 'fall back into fear'. After that night, I knew there would be no going back. I had been living in the shadows, barely surviving each day by just escaping the men in the white coats by the 'skin of my teeth'. Over time I have read this verse again and again, and it gives me confidence that there is no going back to that dark time. I have received the spirit of adoption as a daughter, which was more confirmation for me that I am a child of God. I have always thought about how special an adopted child is. In the process of adoption in this country, not only does the family gain a new member, but that new member is chosen for that family. The adoption authorities, the experts in this procedure, carefully monitor everything, and the child who is selected is the one who is perfect for that family. In Roman times, an adopted son was the heir to the family's estate just as a natural child would be. Even if the family went on to have natural children, the adoptive child would be equal heirs with them. Adoption was not taken lightly in New Testament times and so, when the word adoption is used here in Romans, it shows the reader just how important the Father/Son relationship is. I had been adopted by God himself, and other passages showed how I was chosen,

'But you are a chosen race, a royal priesthood,
a holy nation, a people for his own possession, that
you may proclaim the excellences' of him
who called you out of darkness into his
marvellous light'.'
(1 Peter 2:9 ESV)

This verse gives me great assurance of who I am in God. It could almost be a war cry to warn the enemy not to mess with me.

A great big **WARNING KEEP OUT** sign for Satan.

I AM chosen!
I AM Royalty!
I AM one of God's Children!
I Belong to Him!
I Proclaim His Supremacy!
Darkness you are my Enemy!
I Stand Strong in His Glorious light!
STAY AWAY!

I know the enemy is the master of deception, but he must be deceiving himself if he believes he can mess with this Christian. Knowing that I am a child of God gave me confidence and strength; doubting myself gave the enemy a foothold in my life. This is not something that I should forget in a hurry, but the post-it notes that I placed in my Bible are still there and, when I doubt who I am, even for a second, I can return to them recalling this night again and again. My question to God was, 'how did I get into this state in the first place?' I found my answer in Scripture.

'But no one can enter a strong man's house and
plunder his goods, unless he first binds the
strong man. Then indeed he may
plunder his house.'
(Mark 3:27 ESV)

Imagine a house where a table is laid out with the most amazing feast. The thief cannot resist the opportunity to steal everything on that table because it looks so good. The owner is one of the strongest men on earth and the security system is state-of-the-art, so it wouldn't be easy to gain entry to steal from this table. The owner, however, understands the value of the feast and never leaves it unattended, and so the thief comes up with a plan. The thief befriends the strong man and gains an invitation to the feast. His idea is that he would con the owner in order to steal everything on the table. In fact, now that the thief is inside the house he sees treasures beyond his wildest dreams. The clever thief understands that the owner is too strong for him, so he tells the owner stories about the food so that it wouldn't look so attractive, and the owner stops eating from the table. Weakened with hunger, the thief overpowers him and binds his new friend so tightly to a chair that there is no way to stop the robbery. The thief takes his time and casually removes everything from the house, and the owner, bound and gagged, has lost his ability to stop the thief. The subdued owner, his strength diminished through hunger and thirst and bound by the lies and deception of this so-called friend, can no longer reach anything on the banqueting table, so he admits defeat and no longer tries to eat from the table. He then allows the friend to remove the treasures that were given to him as he passively exists on what the friend feeds him.

That's how I felt at that moment - that I had passively allowed myself to be manipulated by the enemy. I could see the feast, but I couldn't touch it or gain nourishment from it. My friend (the enemy), whom I had invited to the feast, had worn me down with lies and deceptions. The promises God had given me were still the same, but the fact was I no longer had faith in the word of God that fed me. As I said earlier, I had doubted that God could keep His promises, and while I was reading the Word I was ad-libbing. When I didn't believe the things I read, I put them into a box labelled 'Not Written for Me'. Eventually I had stopped reading my Bible altogether, starving myself of the sustenance that I needed. I saw things that were not really there, and my imagination ran riot when there was any chance that I would believe a real truth. The lies that bound me for years were not strong; they were only holding me back because I allowed them to. Each treasure and promise that I had been given had been removed piece by piece without any resistance from me. I had been overpowered by a thief and I had forgotten that my strength was in God.

'The joy of the Lord is my strength' Neh 8:10

I had forgotten who I was and I didn't recognise the enemy, and even the Chinese philosopher knew the outcome of that combination. The full quote from Sun Tzu says this,

"If you know the enemy and know yourself, you need not fear the result of a hundred battles. If you know yourself but not the enemy, for every victory gained you will also suffer a defeat. If you know neither the enemy nor yourself, you will succumb in every battle."

How wise was this man? I had lost every battle for years. I had been living in total defeat, but now there was a bright shining light that I could see at the end of this dark tunnel I was living in. For the first time, I wasn't even suspicious that the light at the end of this tunnel was an express train coming towards me.

Again Jesus spoke to them, saying, "I am the light of the world. Whoever follows me will not walk in darkness, but will have the light of life."
(John 8:12 ESV)

I didn't have to walk in this darkness any longer and I knew it. I had always known it, I had just buried it so deeply that I had forgotten. How did I know it was always there? Jesus said that He is the light of the world I am justified through Christ Jesus:

'Therefore, since we have been justified by faith, we have peace with God through our Lord Jesus Christ.'
(Romans 5:1 ESV)

47

John explains that the darkness cannot overcome the light. I might have been blinded in the dark for a long time, but the light had never gone out, although I had been deceived into believing it wasn't there.

> *'The light shines in the darkness, and the darkness has not overcome it.'*
> *(John 1:5 ESV)*

Jesus my Saviour is the light that lives in me; of this I have no doubt. The truth is in black and white as I read my Bible it is right there for all to see.

> *'I have been crucified with Christ. It is no longer I who live, but Christ who lives in me. And the life I now live in the flesh I live by faith in the Son of God, who loved me and gave himself for me.'*
> *(Galatians 2:19 ESV)*

I may have lost a lot of battles in the past, but God was showing me how to fight. He was starting to even out the score; and we may have been sitting at 3-2 to Satan at that moment, but there is so much more that God had in store for me that night.

> *'No, in all these things we have complete victory through him who loved us!'*
> *(Romans 8:37 NET)*

Mr Sun Tzu's wise words were true - I did not know my enemy and I did not know myself, and I had lost every battle for the last few years. But now I was gaining the advantage. God had shown me who my enemy was and He had shown me who I was. Next on God's agenda that night was to show me my allies. There was more to this battle than even Sun Tzu could ever understand, and while his words of wisdom might have ended there, thankfully God's did not.

Chapter 4
Knowing God

'Then sings my soul my Saviour God to Thee,
How great Thou art,
How great Thou art'.
Carl Gustav Boberg

This was my granny's favourite hymn. She used to make me sing it like a party piece when I was a child. Although it was her favourite hymn she wasn't really a church-goer, as far as I remember, but this song impacted her in some way as it delighted her no end when I sung it. I remember as an adult sitting with her in the hospital just before she passed away. She didn't know I was there, nor had she spoken or even opened her eyes for weeks, and I had no idea what to say next. As I sat in the silence of the small side-ward where she lay, I started to sing. Slowly and a little bit awkwardly at first, as I felt a bit ridiculous singing by myself, I sang 'How Great Thou Art' just because she liked it. The powerful words that I hadn't sung in years suddenly impacted me in a way that I hadn't experienced before.

O LORD my God! When I in awesome wonder
Consider all the works Thy hand hath made;
I see the stars, I hear the mighty thunder,
Thy power throughout the universe displayed:

Then sings my soul, my Saviour God, to Thee,
How great Thou art! How great Thou art!
Then sings my soul, my Saviour God, to Thee,
How great Thou art! How great Thou art!

Tears streamed down my face this time as I sung, partly because I was sitting at the deathbed of the woman who had taught me the hymn, but mainly because I just loved the truth of what I was singing. While I had found it so irritating as a child having to sing this song, now it was such a privilege to sing as I knew the God I was singing about personally. At this point a nurse came in and asked if it was me who was singing. I had forgotten what time it was, 11.30 pm, and there were other patients to consider. I started to apologise for not thinking when the nurse stopped me. She said that some of the patients at the end of the corridor could not hear properly and asked if I could sing a bit louder. So I did, I took my granny's hand and boldly sang all four verses and all four choruses without music. In the eerie silence the air became thick with the presence of God. Now, how to describe that presence is difficult; but there was a peace that came with it, an understanding that, in all of the emotion endured during these final days of watching my granny die, this was not the end. There was a comfort and reassurance that we were not alone in that room. That, to me, was experiencing who God is and at that moment I knew His presence.

I knew that this would be a moment that I would never forget. I knew at that moment who God was because I was experiencing His presence. I don't believe that it was just me who noticed that He was there in that room. I know that God was able to reach my granny in her unconscious state, even though we had not been able to for weeks. As the words floated down the corridor that night, I believe others experienced it too. They heard a hymn that gave an insight into the awesome wonder of God. I may not be a preacher, but God can still use my voice to communicate who He is. All of this was possible because as a little girl my granny taught me her favourite hymn. I spent the next few hours just sitting with her, holding her hand and praying for peace for her. She passed away two days later and we sang this hymn at her funeral. I never knew why it was her favourite hymn, but I know

Then sings my soul My Saviour God to Thee

why it is mine. It is more than a few words put to a nice tune or a fond memory of my grandmother. It is a poem of worship, of understanding who God is and of thanksgiving; a story of love that was poured out for me, as I am reminded of the sacrifice on the cross; and the truth that this song brings when I hear it has reminded me that my soul really does sing for joy.

When God said 'know who I am' as He spoke to me that night in my bedroom, I had no notion of how the knowledge of who God is would be the mightiest weapon of all in my quest to find a cure for my depression. Because that was what that evening of studying the Word and conversation with God had become. It had started with one phrase 'know your enemy'. That phrase led to hope as I began to listen to what God was saying, and now His voice was so clear that my desire to know Him and His way was increasing by the minute. Remember, I wasn't looking for a cure when this began in the car I was looking for a way out but now it was almost midnight and the thoughts of a way out had been removed completely from my mind. I was inspired and excited by what I had read and heard, and I was motivated by a will to live that I hadn't experienced in a long time. God had more for me, and as excited as I was, I needed to listen carefully so as not to miss anything.

Sun Tzu was a military strategist in earthly battles; on the other hand, we fight against principalities and powers. This is why I needed to understand the God I serve. I had forgotten just how mighty and powerful God was. I had assumed that God judged and loved based on my limitations as a human. I had presumed that He behaved towards me the way I would have behaved towards others, and my expectations of Him had not been too high lately, considering my experiences in the world of depression. I didn't consider myself of any worth, why then would God? God could choose anyone else. I mean, take a look around, God, there are more deserving people than me. Why don't you just give up on me? I have. Isn't that what Moses asked God to do when God gave him the task of going back to Egypt to liberate His people from slavery? Moses had many excuses - I don't speak well, what if they don't believe me and eventually he said, 'Lord use someone else'. All of this after he had seen the burning bush, the staff turn into a snake and the diseased hand healed. God had even told him his name; 'I AM', 'I am the God of Abraham, Isaac and Jacob', and Moses still doubted.

'God said to Moses, "I AM WHO I AM." And he
said, "Say this to the people of Israel,
'I AM has sent me to you.'"
(Exodus 3:14 ESV)

Anna's God and the I AM the God of Abraham don't match up. My God has been limited by every experience that I have ever had of people, but I, like Moses, had experienced the presence of God on more than one occasion and I still doubted. I knew that I needed to see God in a different way. God is Holy, not like any other human. Yes, we are created in His image, but that doesn't mean He is like us or behaves like us. Defining the Holiness of God is difficult as it doesn't translate well in any language, but it is a word that describes God throughout scripture. God is completely separate from everything else that exists. How can anyone know who He is? Experience and knowledge! Wasn't that what this whole night was becoming? An experience that I would never forget and the knowledge was clearly written for me in the Bible. John explains what Jesus told him about God,

'This is the message we have heard from Him and
proclaim to you, that God is light, and in Him
is no darkness at all.'
(1 John 1:5 ESV)

That's how I am reminded that God is different. There is no darkness in Him at all, so how can God behave towards me the way people do? There is certainly darkness in this world and there was certainly darkness in me, I felt, but it clearly says in John that in Him there is no darkness. That means that God can't be limited, as we are, because He is Holy and completely separate from us. But that doesn't make Him inaccessible to us. Moses spoke to Him and I am speaking to Him. He is talking me through this process of understanding this battle against depression. He is taking the time for me to find a victory in all of this misery, which means that He still wants a personal relationship with me. Crazy or not, I haven't put Him off.

God is faithful. I have heard this tagged on to the end of many conversations when people don't know what to say about a situation. If someone is so ill that there is no hope, God is faithful. If the sale of a house falls through, God is faithful. If an earthquake destroys a whole town and kills half of the population, God is faithful. I hear this phrase tossed around without explanation by unbelievers and believers alike. We are back to the Christianese again - people throw around true statements about God without ever truly understanding their meaning. Clichés are phrases that are over-used and that over-use diminishes the authority of the original thought. I myself had become guilty of this. I am finally understanding His faithfulness as He rescues me from the darkness of depression and suicidal thoughts. So now when I say to someone, 'God is faithful', I say it with purpose and intent to influence that person with the truth of God.

I know God is faithful because the Bible says:

'the Lord is faithful. He will establish you and guard
you against the evil one'
(2 Thessalonians 3:3)

God is faithful is not a throwaway statement for the sake of comfort - I say it because I have inside knowledge. That night, God wanted to show me who He was so that I understood who was on my side. The Creator who said, 'let there be light' was on my side. Not only does God not live in the darkness, He was not prepared to leave me there. We remove the power of these words by using them so frivolously. God is faithful and He is holy, and defining who God is, although it is hard to do, was crucial to the healing of my mind.

For what seemed to be an eternity, I had lived in what I can only call a tormented state. Nothing made sense, so how did I know that this conversation that I was having with this particular voice was the real God? I knew because it was gentle and calm and down-to-earth. For the first time in a long time there was no screaming in my head. The Message Bible describes so well how God was rescuing me that night.

'Are you tired? Worn out? Burned out on religion?
Come to me. Get away with me and you'll recover
your life. I'll show you how to take a real rest.
Walk with me and work with me—watch how I do
it. Learn the unforced rhythms of grace. I won't lay
anything heavy or ill-fitting on you. Keep company
with me and you'll learn to live freely and lightly.'
(Matthew 11:28-30 The Message)

God had said, 'come to me', and I had answered that call. What captured me was that, although a few hours ago I thought I couldn't cope, now there was renewed determination. 'I won't lay anything ill-fitting on you' or 'my yoke is easy my burden is light'-whichever way you want to put it-caught me. What I had been experiencing during this whole bout of depression was neither easy nor light; it weighed heavy every day and I knew that this was not from God nor was it His will for my life. He would not have reached out to me and brought me to this Scripture if He had wanted me to stay in a place of oppression. I considered again God's message: Come to me, learn the unforced rhythms of grace. I know you are burnt out and tired, I am here to rescue you. I have so much to show you. Let's take a walk and I will tell you all about My grace. Only when you truly know Me will you understand how to move through trials like these. I am committed to you for the duration of your life. Continue to walk with me and together we will endure. The unforced rhythms of grace helped me to understand that this grace is as easy as breathing and should be a natural part of every Christian's life. As we approach any battle we should not be looking for that grace because it is already there. With this in mind then we can stand strong on the Word as it prepares us for battle.

> *'Be strong and courageous. Do not fear or be in dread of them, for it is the LORD your God who goes with you. He will not leave you or forsake you.'*
> *(Deuteronomy 31:1 ESV)*

Moses was persuading the Israelites to take courage as they entered the promised land, and I knew that God was promising me the same thing - a life that would be completely different if I trusted Him. He would not leave me. You see, I didn't need to call on God as back-up in a fight and get a bit roughed-up while I held the fort until He arrived. He was already there the whole time. The unforced rhythm of His grace is what sustains me from the beginning of the battle to the end.

Come to me and I will give you rest

Tonight I understood that I had been held hostage by the depression, but that the situation had changed as I had been extracted from the enemy's camp as God kept His promise never to leave me.

God now had my undivided attention. I know who
God is because the Bible tells me who He is.

I also know who God is because I have experienced
His presence in the bad times and also in the good. As
I sit alone praying or while listening to the preaching
and teaching of others, I have known that He is with
me. For me to give a great theological revelation of
how to know God would not make any sense, as how
I know God will not be how you know Him. There
is no formula to knowing God, there is no system
to follow. Four worship songs and a sermon on a
Sunday morning will not help you know who God is.
Unless you are seeking Him and walking with Him
in every aspect of your life, you will not truly know
how your life corresponds to His purpose for you. I
had kept God at arm's length during this period of my
life because I did not have any notion of who He was.
Contrary to that thought, I began to write down the
many words that I knew would describe God: 'Creator
of the Universe', 'King above all kings', 'Sovereign
Lord', 'Living God', 'God of Peace', 'King of Glory'
holy, divine, faithful, powerful, gracious, merciful,
omnipotent and omniscient, righteous, forgiving,
healer, Father, husband, friend. I have read about
these descriptions in the Bible and heard about them
as others have experienced them and testified to their
accuracy. But to truly know God for yourself, you
must seek Him for yourself, no-one can do it for you.
Getting to know Him during times of peace helps us

prepare to do battle with confidence, it doesn't mean we never have to do battle again.

'No temptation has overtaken you that is not common to man. God is faithful, and he will not let you be tempted beyond your ability, but with the temptation he will also provide the way of escape, that you may be able to endure it.'
(1 Corinthians 10:13 ESV)

This scripture is another reminder of the promise of God in Paul's letter to the Corinthians. The Bible is full of these assurances, and I had been so distracted that I was unable to recall what I had read. I knew after reading this that, not only would I be a depression-survivor, I would wage war on it for the rest of my life, not just for me but for the sake of others too. I would reveal the deception and express in whatever way I could how knowing God is the only way. I can of course battle the principalities and powers of this world, knowing my enemy and knowing who I am in Him, and these would be significant strategies in any war scenario, but without knowing God Himself the victory would be an empty one. All I would gain would be my sanity, which without God is no sanity at all.

"There is nothing that comes my way that I can't survive"

I felt so much regret for time wasted at this point. I missed my relationship with God. How had I not seen this before? The enemy would have me believe that I wasn't really saved in the first place. Doesn't the Bible talk about false converts? Was I one of those? I don't believe so, and this is why: Paul in his letter to the Galatians asks,

'Who has impeded your progress and kept you from obeying the truth? You were off to such a good start. I know for certain the pressure isn't coming from God. He keeps calling you to the truth. You know what they say, "Just a little yeast causes all the dough to rise," so even the slightest detour from the truth will take you to a destination you do not desire.'
(Galatians 5:7-9 The Voice)

Like the Galatian converts I had started off well, I thought, but my regret now was wasting time lamenting in my own misery. I did not desire a life without God, I never had. Ignoring the sacrifice that Jesus had made, and living without the Spirit of God in me, fills me with great sorrow and regret, but I knew that I was not a false convert. I knew God and I had some knowledge of who He was through the scriptures, and this truth gave me strength even in the times when I hadn't recognised it. I had read the scriptures and experienced His presence and now, because of that foundation, I was being rescued.

*'But as for you, continue in what you have learned
and have firmly believed, knowing from whom you
learned it and how from childhood you have been
acquainted with the sacred writings, which are
able to make you wise for salvation through faith in
Christ Jesus. All Scripture is breathed out by God
and profitable for teaching, for reproof,
for correction, and for training in righteousness,
that the man of God may be complete, equipped for
every good work.'*
(2 Timothy 3:1 ESV)

I might have taken a detour in my Christian walk, but, because the promises of God were written on my heart, I knew that all I had to do was turn to Him as He had never left me. My objective now was to know Him in a deeper way so that I could stand firm in the certainty of who He is.

The enemy had killed, stolen and destroyed. I now knew my enemy, knew myself, and I knew God. The score was now a draw, 3-3. In sporting terms this game could go either way. But I knew God had more for me and I didn't need to worry about the score anymore because it was an obvious win that I hadn't experienced in a long time.

Have you ever sat up all night catching up with friends or family, reminiscing about old times or filling in the gaps because it has been so long since you spent time with that person? God now had my undivided attention. I truly did not want this night to end. There was so much I needed to know and so much I wanted to talk about. Thankfully, God wasn't finished there; and in the small hours, I became reacquainted with my first love as we continued in the pursuit of truth, not fantasy. Mark was asleep beside me now and the business of the day was gone as the house was still. My next words I said quietly so as not to wake anyone. My first prayer of any substance to my God in years.

'Create in me a clean heart, O God, and renew a right spirit within me. Cast me not away from your presence, and take not your Holy Spirit from me. Restore to me the joy of your salvation, and renew a right spirit within me.'
(Psalms 51:10-12 ESV)

God granted my request.

Chapter 5
Knowing Jesus

And on the way Jesus asked his disciples,
"Who do people say that I am?"
(Mark 8:27 ESV)

On a visit to India in 2007, I was a witness to a miracle. We were visiting a village to distribute food when a woman came to the leaders. She was pointing at her mouth, and at first I thought that she wanted food that was of course why we were there. Looking around, there were so many hungry people. The charity we were with came to this place once a week and gave out boiled eggs and bananas. We were told that this would be the only food that they were sure of getting; anything else that these people ate throughout the week would have been scavenged for in bins. Yet offering her food was not what she wanted; as hungry as she was, she had no interest in the food. Someone who knew her explained that she couldn't speak, she had never been able to speak. This lady had come to the leaders believing that they had the answer to this problem, and of course they did. In order for her to speak, they would take this to the Father and pray for her in the name of Jesus Christ. The pastors began to pray. I watched, my heart in my mouth, as I could see the desperation in the face of this woman. What happened next I would not have believed if I hadn't seen it with my own eyes. Not only did the woman speak, but the first word she said was 'Jesus'. Miracles of Biblical proportions really do happen. I had witnessed this one and, believe me, there were many more on that trip that I also witnessed. I understood the healing power of Jesus and I was now wondering how I could have forgotten so easily what I had experienced in India.

I had seen first-hand the hope in the Indian woman's eyes and I had mistaken it for desperation. So quickly I had forgotten the endless possibilities if I just had faith. I had become short-sighted, not seeing beyond the end of my own nose, not seeing beyond the here and now. I am reminded in Mark 8 that I am not the only one with a short memory; even the disciples forgot what they had seen from one minute to another. They had watched Jesus feeding the five thousand and then worried about not having anything to eat because they had forgotten to bring bread. I had seen amazing miracles in India when I visited with the church, yet I had been completely consumed by the fear that my insanity was beyond a miracle.

I began to read about Jesus that night, reminding myself of who He really is. Starting at the beginning of His ministry, I realised that Jesus understood the enemy. His ministry began with an encounter with the enemy after fasting for forty days and forty nights. Jesus was taken into the desert and was tempted by Satan, who had used three different tactics to tempt Jesus. The first one was using the weakness of hunger. Humans need to eat and so, knowing that Jesus was hungry after His fast, the temptation to turn the stones into bread would be a hard one for any human to resist. Jesus responded with words taken from Deuteronomy 8:3,

'But he answered, "It is written, "'Man shall not
live by bread alone, but by every word that
comes from the mouth of God.'"
(Matthew 4:4 ESV)

The second temptation appealed to one of the worst characteristics of man - his ego. I can imagine it now, 'Sure you know who you are, Jesus; you could throw yourself down and the very angels would tend to you.' Can you imagine a human being having the power that Jesus had and not being tempted by this? Everyone would see that He truly was the Son of God - what an ego boost that would be in the world today. The devil knew who He was and Jesus knew who he was, but at this point the world did not. How easy it would have been to reveal His identity. The people would have fallen at his feet and worshipped Him; and he would have avoided the horror of the sacrifice that He later would have to make. Wouldn't that have made more sense? Thankfully it was not one of us: it was Jesus who was being subject to these particular temptations. Jesus again addressed this temptation with scripture from the Psalms 91: 11-12,

'Jesus said to him, "Again it is written, 'You shall
not put the Lord your God to the test.'"
(Matthew 4:7 ESV)

The final temptation was appealing to one of man's greatest downfalls, the enticement of power. "I will give you everything that you see if you will fall down and worship me." Don't we live in a world where power is the most sought-after commodity? It is certainly the one thing for which men are prepared to sell their souls. But everything that the devil was offering was already Jesus' mission. What the devil was offering was another way a way that was not the purpose and plan of God and would be without suffering. Jesus replied again with scripture from Deuteronomy 6:13.

'Then Jesus said to him, "Be gone, Satan! For it is written, "'You shall worship the Lord your God and him only shall you serve.'"
(Matthew 4:10 ESV)

I had read this passage in Matthew many times, but, until that night in my room, I never really considered the impact of Jesus as a human walking this earth. I had never really considered that He had experienced what I had. As a man He would have felt the desire to help Himself in all of these temptations. He must have identified with the compulsion to fix His hunger, the desire that He must have felt as the enemy goaded Him into revealing His true identity, and finally the proposal of more power. What human could resist any of this? I am not sure, even now, that I wouldn't be tempted. As a Christian, you hope you would make better choices, but how many of us really do? The Bible says,

'For we do not have a high priest who is unable to sympathize with our weaknesses, but one who in every respect has been tempted as we are, yet without sin.'
(Hebrews 4:15 ESV)

The thing that caught my attention most when I read this was not just that Jesus had been tempted in His weakest moments, but I was focusing on how Jesus knew exactly how to resist these temptations. He spoke the word of God. He didn't just quote some scriptures He had learned in the temple; these words were written in His heart. We are told a story that explains how Mary and Joseph, after frantically searching for their lost son, had found Him in the temple. Jesus was quite unperturbed by the anxiety of His parents and said, 'did you not know I would be in my Father's house?' Jesus from a young age wanted to be absorbed in the scriptures. Unfortunately, I was not as zealous for the scriptures; and in fact, even as an adult, my lacklustre

"I had for too long forgotten what I believed and whom I believed"

attitude to learn from the Bible left a lot to be desired. However, without the Word of God, how would I gain the confidence to engage in battle? It seems so obvious now - and hind-sight is a wonderful thing - but the more I read the Word of God, the more I want to read. The desire grows, but unfortunately at this point in my story, this desire had left me; and even though I went to church twice a week, my Bible had been gathering dust for a long time. My manual had been sitting on a shelf and I had neglected to consult it. I was beginning to appreciate the amount of God's Word that I was remembering that night, although I regret that I did not have more. The Bible stories that I was taught in Sunday School, the scriptures that I had memorised for Bible class and for my GB badges, and even the Apostles' Creed (although it wasn't scripture) I had committed to memory so that I wouldn't forget what I believed - they were all coming back to me now.

'I believe in God the Father Almighty, Maker of heaven and earth: And in Jesus Christ his only Son our Lord, who was conceived by the Holy Ghost; Born of the Virgin Mary, suffered under Pontius Pilate, was crucified, dead, and buried: He descended into hell. On the third day He rose again from the dead; He ascended into heaven, and sits on the right hand of God the Father Almighty; From thence he shall come to judge the quick and the dead. I believe in the Holy Ghost; the holy catholic church. The Communion of Saints and the forgiveness of sins. The Resurrection of the body and the life everlasting.
Amen.'

I am so thankful to Reverend Tom Crabbe for teaching me the Creed during confirmation class. That class led to my first communion and confirmation into the church. All of the teaching that had influenced my life until this point had led me to a place where I could fully understand the commitment I was making to live a life for Jesus, even though I was only a child then. I knew what I believed and, under the conviction of the Holy Spirit, I repented of my sins and accepted Jesus as my Lord and Saviour at a youth fellowship weekend in Newcastle [Northern Ireland] at the age of fifteen. Later in life, even in my madness I had been going every week to Bible school and attending church meetings (keeping up appearances, of course). The word of God was taught and I had taken some of it in. Thanks to the passion and devotion of those leaders in my early years and thanks to the commitment and dedication of the leaders in the church I attend now, I was exposed to the things of God even if I was an apathetic attender; they were faithful. These stories and scriptures were all part of me, just as the scriptures came so naturally to Jesus when He was tempted. The more I read my Bible that night, the more I wanted to know how Jesus handled His encounters with the enemy.

I knew the stories where Jesus had healed the sick and raised the dead. The deaf heard, the blind saw, the lame walked - all were healed and restored to a normal life. I had been so engrossed in covering up my depression that I had not considered the possibility that I could be healed. Jesus healed the physical, I

73

had seen it happen in others and experienced it in my own life. If my depression had only been a chemical imbalance, merely a physical ailment, then why did I not believe that God would heal me? Wouldn't it be another blind person seeing, or lame person walking, instead He would just fix my brain.

As I was discovering, through God revealing to me that night through His Word, depression was not just a physical problem. I had come to understand that, not only had I neglected to know my enemy, I had also neglected to know my Saviour. Jesus was like an acquaintance in my life - a friend I met at church twice a week and whose diary I read every now and again as I enjoyed the tales that are told in the Bible. I stuck to the pleasant stories about blind Bartimaeus being able to see and the time when Jesus stopped the adulterous woman from being stoned to death, the Jesus who raised Jairus' daughter from the dead and spoke in parables in order to help people who trust in Him to understand the principles of Christianity. My Jesus was a good man who came so that I could be forgiven and go to heaven I avoided anything I didn't understand and side-stepped anything that didn't make me feel good.

That night in my room, I read a few of the other stories that I usually tended to avoid in a bid to understand how Jesus handled His encounters with the enemy. One of the first pieces of interesting information that

I learned was that the enemy knew who Jesus was and was fully aware of His authority over him.

> *'And immediately there was in their synagogue a*
> *man with an unclean spirit. And he cried out,*
> *"What have you to do with us, Jesus of Nazareth?*
> *Have you come to destroy us? I know who you are--*
> *the Holy One of God."*
> *(Mark 1:22-24 ESV)*

In this story in Mark's Gospel, Jesus and the disciples had gone into the temple because it was the Sabbath. The man with the unclean spirit knew that Jesus spoke with the authority of God. As the onlookers watched Jesus deal with the unclean spirit, they recognised the authority by which He spoke and they were amazed! There were many more stories of Jesus' encounters with Satan.

In the Gospels of Matthew, Mark and Luke, all describe the same story of a man who, we are told, was demon-possessed or who had an unclean spirit. We are told that this man had become so influenced by evil spirits that he had to be shackled because he was fierce and violent and no one could pass by him. This man was so tormented that he wore no clothes and, when the unclean spirit took hold, he had so much strength that even the chains that bound him could not hold him and he broke free from them and terrorised the people. In Mark, we are told how the unclean spirit tormented the man so much he that cried out and cut himself with stones. It occurred to me, when I read about this man, that he was so manipulated by these demons that he chose to harm himself. Although I had thought many times about ending it all as my mind was tormented, I didn't harm myself. However, I have certainly heard of people who become so depressed and emotionally strung-out that they self-harm by cutting themselves, usually with razor blades or knives. Thinking now about all the behaviours that could be mental disorders classed as mental illness - self-harming being one of them - could, then, the everyday struggles that are now accepted as normal also be doors that open us up to the enemy? For example, drink or drug addiction, even eating disorders and gambling - all of these consume the sufferer just like depression. We become prey to the obsession to eat or not eat, drink, take drugs or self-harm, and all the while the enemy takes hold of our weakened state, and forms strongholds in the mind that we find hard to break down or move away from. Guilt, confusion and shame at our weakness kicks in, and suddenly the enemy that we ignore is running riot through our minds and we believe that it is always going to be this way because that's just how it is. We are our own worst enemies - too proud to believe in the superstitious nonsense comes to mind. I am in control of my own destiny - 'there is no fate but what we make' (from The Terminator movie for those who don't recognise the quote).

To the enlightened man the supernatural is classed as superstitious nonsense. This is a great big fat lie of the devil, and I make no apologies about saying it. I know that to believe that you are influenced by something spiritual could get you locked up in a looney bin nowadays. Let's face it, depression, self-harming, hearing voices and emotional turmoil are not new. Two thousand years ago Jesus dealt with these things as He came up against them, and, each time, the spirits that influenced the person, recognised Him and feared because they knew their fate. This was not a parlour trick to entertain the people, this was a reality for the man whom Jesus healed and for the many others who came after who suffered from these debilitating influences on their lives.

When Jesus spoke to the man He asked the unclean spirit his name. It answered, "Legion for we are many." Legion was one of the biggest units that the Roman armies were measured in at the time, so this name gave an idea to just how big the influence of these demons had become. Knowing what was about to become of them, they begged Jesus not to send them out into the abyss. This highlighted the supernatural struggle between Jesus and Satan. Satan's goal is to control us in any way that he can.

"Legion - a division of 3000-6000 in the acient Roman army"

Jesus, on the other hand, came to set us free from sin and the influence of Satan. However, we have become so free-thinking and progressive that we have developed an intolerance for the uneducated mumbo jumbo of the supernatural, and, we have accepted the idea that we are at the mercy of these illnesses, and, so we wait for a medical cure, or at least a pill, that will curb the symptoms for a while. This doesn't seem very enlightened to me to ignore the remedy that we were given two thousand years ago in favour of a modern medicine.

If we are given accounts of this story in three different gospels by the eye witnesses of the ministry of Christ, then why on earth would we think that we know better? This story is here for a reason, and for me that night it was revealing to me the simple answer to my depression: JESUS. Not only did Jesus lead his disciples by displaying the authority of God, He also gave them the authority to do the same.

'And when he had called unto him his twelve disciples, he gave them power against unclean spirits, to cast them out, and to heal all manner of sickness and all manner of disease. And as ye go, preach, saying, 'The kingdom of heaven is at hand. Heal the sick, cleanse the lepers, raise the dead, cast out devils: freely ye have received, freely give.' (Matthew 10:1, 7-8 KJV)

This is confirmed in Luke 9:1-6 and Mark 6:7,13 each disciple retelling the instructions he was given.

But, not only did Jesus give the disciples these instructions and the authority to carry them out, He also left them for us.

'And he said to them, "Go into all the world and proclaim the gospel to the whole creation. Whoever believes and is baptized will be saved, but whoever does not believe will be condemned. And these signs will accompany those who believe: in my name they will cast out demons; they will speak in new tongues; they will pick up serpents with their hands; and if they drink any deadly poison, it will not hurt them; they will lay their hands on the sick, and they will recover."
(Mark 16:15-18 ESV)

There was so much more to discover as I read that night about Jesus, and I became so inspired that I am not really sure what order it all came in. However, I came across this story in Mark's Gospel as I read that night and it made me realise that, with all my intelligence and common sense, I was not thinking clearly. I had been trapped in a mind-set of rational, logical thinking and I dared not step outside of that box. I had limited my understanding to the knowledge of the doctors, and faith and trust in Jesus was separate from this part of my life. I needed to believe and have faith.

There was a young man who was brought to Jesus by his father to be healed, and Jesus commanded the deaf and dumb spirit to come out of him. A spirit had caused him to be deaf and dumb and to convulse so badly that it threw him into the fire and into the water to destroy him. The father explained this to Jesus. This was a perfect example that faith and belief is not about having a positive mental attitude. This man desired so much to have his son healed and, although we are not told it here, he had probably sought many solutions to his son's problems, as anyone who is a parent would understand. Here, when Jesus says all things are possible to him who believes, the father understands that his belief is not enough nor has it ever been enough. The father then replies 'Lord I believe; help my unbelief.' Faith is a gift from God. and no matter how much faith we have we are not self-sufficient. Again, a positive mental attitude is not the answer here. We must have faith and believe in the person Jesus. How arrogant has the human race become that we wholeheartedly believe that we have evolved so much that we can exist without the one who created us? The Bible says,

'For by grace you have been saved through faith. And this is not your own doing; it is the gift of God, not a result of works, so that no one may boast. For we are his workmanship, created in Christ Jesus for good works, which God prepared beforehand, that we should walk in them.'
(Ephesians 2:8-10 ESV)

I began this chapter with a verse from Mark's Gospel chapter 9 in which Jesus asks the disciples, 'Who do people say that I am?' The disciples answer Him with the rumours that were heard among the people that He was John the Baptist or Elijah or one of the other prophets. So I asked myself the same question, 'Who do people say that Jesus is?' 'Jesus was just a man', I have heard many people say, or he was half man half god like the Greek myths of Hercules. 'He was just a religious fanatic who existed a long time ago who believed he was the Messiah.'

Then Jesus went on to ask the disciples, 'who do you say that I am?' and Peter answered 'you are the Christ'. I believe the answer that Peter gave. The Bible clearly tells us in Colossians who Jesus is: He is the creator, and His death on a cross was for us - His creation. He lived and died to reconcile us to Him, and there is no man on earth who would have willingly given his life to rescue us. He was not a fraud or a myth, nor was He just a man. He was divine, and the Bible clearly tells us this.

'He has delivered us from the domain of darkness and transferred us to the kingdom of his beloved Son, in whom we have redemption, the forgiveness of sins. He is the image of the invisible God, the firstborn of all creation. For by him all things were created, in heaven and on earth, visible and invisible, whether thrones or dominions or rulers

or authorities - all things were created through him
and for him. And he is before all things, and in him
all things hold together.'
(Colossians 1:13-17 ESV)

The disciples knew who Jesus was, and I know who Jesus is, and the Bible tells us that even the enemy knows and exclaims that Jesus is the 'Holy One of God' [Luke 4:31]. The enemy recognises the authority of Jesus. Where Jesus is present, the enemy cannot stay for long. The darkness cannot overcome the light. The enemy is happy to invade our weaknesses at every opportunity, and just because we are Christians does not make us immune to the enemy's schemes. The doubts that had overwhelmed me had been fuelled by the idea that Jesus was holy, a divine heavenly being who didn't really understand the torment of a depressed mind. But we are told in Hebrews 4 that Jesus was able to sympathise with our weaknesses and had been tempted in every respect, just as we are. I remembered Lewis (my Pastor) talking about how Jesus was also tormented and oppressed in the garden of Gethsemane. This story was the next one to come to mind that night.

I have spoken about the darkness that I felt had surrounded me in the times of deepest depression. I remember during one of the many counselling sessions being so sure that no-one could possibly understand the pressure of this anxiety that weighed so heavily. If you could physically see it on my back, I would be bent double like an old woman of ninety with arthritis. I heard the words spoken that day that Jesus knew the pressure I was under and He had experienced the anxiety that I had, if not more. But, in all of my lovely Sunday school stories, I have never heard about a stressed Jesus and certainly not a depressed one. The pastor turned to the book of Luke and read to me about the night that Jesus agonised in the garden at Gethsemane. I thought I knew

John names him Malchus the servant of the high priest Caiaphas.

this story when Jesus asked the disciples to pray and they fell asleep and Jesus asked God to 'take this cup away from me'. He then said, 'Thy will be done' and then He was betrayed by Judas and, as the Roman soldiers approached, Peter cut off the ear of one of the crowd but Jesus healed him. This might be the outline of the story, but I had missed a crucial point that would help me understand that the darkness that I had faced everyday was nothing compared to the darkness that Jesus experienced closing in on Him.

We don't have the privilege of witnessing this scene for ourselves so, from what I have read in the gospels I would like to look at this passage again. You will find this story in Matthew 26:36-46, Mark 14:32-42 and Luke 22:39-46. In Matthew and Mark's Gospels, we are told that Jesus told the disciples to watch and pray as He went a little bit further into the garden and

He took with Him Peter, James and John. On three occasions He went back to them to find them not keeping watch and praying but sleeping. Matthew and Mark describe Jesus' anxiety using these words,

"My soul is overwhelmed with sorrow to the point of death"
(Matthew 26:38; Mark 14:34 NKJV)

In Luke's Gospel, however, the story varies slightly; and it is there that I find what I believe is detail that was placed there by the writer because it is important for us to understand the humanity of Jesus. Luke says in his account of this story that, as Jesus knelt to pray, an angel appeared to strengthen Him.

'And being in an agony He prayed more earnestly; and His sweat became like great drops of blood falling down to the ground.'
(Luke 22:44 ESV)

I am struck dumb with embarrassment now when I think about how I believed that no-one could possibly imagine how I was feeling. How wrong I was! Jesus really was aware of the darkness that I was living with; in fact, He was more aware of the darkness than I would ever know. He was in agony, Luke says, and He prayed more intently. The word agony or ἀγωνία {ag-o-nee'-ah} in the Greek can translate - severe mental struggles and emotions, agony or anguish. Jesus knew what was coming next. He knew that He would be beaten, scourged and suffer the cruellest and most agonising death that man could ever have conceived. But, worse than that He would carry the weight and punishment of every sin committed and would ever be committed by man. I can only try to imagine the darkness that fell on Jesus during that time. To be under so much pressure that the blood vessels in your sweat glands would burst from stress - is that possible? It turns out that it is. After a little bit of research, I discovered that it is called hematohidrosis. Although this is a rare medical condition, there are recorded instances where people have sweated droplets of blood due to extreme pressure. Never could I conceive in my wildest nightmares the stress that Jesus must have experienced that night.

'Nevertheless, not my will, but yours, be done.'
(Luke 22:42 ESV)

I don't know anyone who would have taken on that mantle and submitted it to the hands of the Father without wanting it to be taken from them. What also stood out for me, as I read verses 43 and 44, is that, even though Jesus submitted these things to God and gained strength from heaven, it goes on to say that He was still in agony. Even in that agony, He continued to pray, conversing with the Father, not running away from Him, but taking every worry and every doubt to Him. Jesus was in constant communion with the Father. I, on the other hand, was not; and the darkness and loneliness that I felt was because I was separated from God due to my sinful nature. Jesus was about to be separated from God, not because of His sinful nature - because we are told that He lived without sin - but because of mine. Jesus surrendered to God's will even under the extreme pressure of His imminent sacrifice. I needed to do the same.

I know who Jesus is, so, with the authority He gave me when I believed and was baptized, I believe and have faith that the enemy can be cast out and that my mind will be restored without harm, just as is reported about the man in the temple [Luke 4:35]. Oh Lord, forgive me, for I am my own worst enemy. I am self-indulgent, self-absorbed and selfish. I think I am so smart and I have all the answers when the only answer is you. You were selfless in Your actions when You surrendered Your will to the Father and I thank You for Your sacrifice. It is time for me to follow Your example and surrender my whole life to God.

There was such a peace in my mind, and I experienced a calmness return to me that had left me so long ago. This was an amazing gift that I was being given and I knew that my mind was being restored completely. I also knew that God was not finished yet and there was a final gift to sustain this wholeness in Him.

Knowledge of the Holy Spirit would complete and re-establish the strongholds of my mind that the enemy had occupied for so long. My sanity had returned, and God was showing me the pathway to sustain it.

Chapter 6
Knowing the Holy Spirit

*'And I will ask the Father, and He will give you
another Helper, to be with you forever, even the
Spirit of truth, whom the world cannot receive,
because it neither sees Him nor knows Him.
You know Him, for He dwells with you and
will be in you.'*
(John 14:16-17 ESV)

Jesus was speaking to His disciples when He made this promise of a Helper to be with us forever. It spoke to me about the promises of Jesus and helped me to remember that I had never been alone, I had just convinced myself that I was. From the age of fifteen I had received salvation and the promise of the Holy Spirit, the Helper, who would be with me forever. Even looking back to the years that I had spent away from God, in my late teens and early twenties when I had thought that the grass was greener on the party scene, I had been prompted many times by the Holy Spirit to return to a life living for God, but I had ignored it. These promptings came by way of hesitance just before doing something stupid and they came through wise warnings from Christian friends. Did this prompting of the Holy Spirit mean that God did not want me to have fun? No! He wanted me to turn from the things that I was doing that He knew would cause me to look at myself with so little value or self-worth in later life. All of those nudges that I had felt when I did something that I knew was wrong, but I did them anyway, would be things that I would have to live with. Those nudges, if I had taken heed of them, could have prevented me from a life time of regrets. I now realise that they were the Helper that I had been promised and I had ignored so arrogantly, thinking I knew better. Sadly, each time I ignored Him, I slipped a little deeper into a world of influence that was harder to come away from.

I had turned my life around by the age of twenty-five. I was married to a good man, had a job and a great family life, so how had I managed to suffer from depression in my late thirties? I had repented again and turned from the wrong path to the right one, but, somewhere in the midst of it all, I hadn't really grasped the idea that I was forgiven because I hadn't forgiven myself. God could and would meet my every need. I never really understood that I was living in the constant presence of God, even though God makes this promise to His people all the way through the Bible. Because I had never really tried to stay connected to God and I had been too self-reliant, I could never truly speak the words of the Psalmist until now.

> 'O Eternal One, You have explored my heart and
> know exactly who I am;
> You even know the small details like when I take a
> seat and when I stand up again.
> Even when I am far away,
> You know what I'm thinking.
> You observe my wanderings and my sleeping, my
> waking and my dreaming,
> and You know everything I do in more detail than
> even I know.'
> (Psalm 139:1-3 the Voice)

There is nowhere that I or anyone can hide from God. I had, on the other hand, been trying to hide from

Him my flawed side. Do you remember when you were a child and your mum knew by the look on your face what you were about to do? Or instinctively she knew to shout when you were in the other room close to the chocolate cake that you were about to take a bite. I used to tell my kids that I could see everything and hear everything, it was like a gift that I got when I became a mum, and that I had eyes in the back of my head. The truth was that I knew them inside and out, and not to go all Mystic Meg about it, I could predict what was going on in their mischievous minds. I knew them - they were my children, and God knew me - I was His child and His creation. He knew everything about me, warts and all. Now, as I read His word and talked to Him, I knew that there was nowhere I could go to hide from Him. Why had I wasted so much energy and time trying to hide? He had been there all along, watching, warning, waiting and guiding through His Holy Spirit.

> *'If I go up into heaven, You are there.*
> *If I make my bed in the realm of the dead,*
> *You are there.*
> *If I ride on the wings of morning,*
> *if I make my home in the most isolated part*
> *of the ocean,*
> *Even then You will be there to guide me;*
> *Your right hand will embrace me,*
> *for You are always there.'*
> *(Psalm 139:8-10 The Voice)*

Even in my backslidden state of depression, He was with me; the Psalmist confirms this. God was always there in my darkest times; and in the times of greatest torment He held me and stopped me from jumping off the ledge into oblivion! What had happened to me that night, when the voice that stopped me in my tracks with the words 'know your enemy', is explained so clearly in John,

I cannot hide from Him. He is always with me.

> *'But the Helper, the Holy Spirit, whom the Father*
> *will send in my name, He will teach you all things*
> *and bring to your remembrance all that*
> *I have said to you.'*
> *(John 14:26 ESV)*

The Holy Spirit had brought to remembrance all the things that I knew from the scriptures, limited as they were, to help me see the truth about my situation. I had the power over my dominating emotions. I also had the power over the influences of the enemy and, because I was ill-equipped for the battle, the enemy had run wild in my mind for too long. The Helper was with me reminding me, teaching me with the Word of God.

> *'But he who is joined to the Lord becomes*
> *one spirit with him.'*
> *(1Corinthians 6:17 ESV)*

At this point, I was becoming a tad fearful that the night would end and I would return to the powerless, tormented state that I had been in at the start of the evening. What if I lost that connection? What if I got a bad signal or there was no network available, just like the mobile phones on which we have become so dependent? Although my confidence was growing in the Word that I read and in the knowledge and revelation that I was being given, I found that the fear factor of regressing was also growing. I wanted to make sure that I never looked back from this moment in time; I needed this revelation to be engrained in my memory so that I would never forget. I remembered a story I had heard in Luke that I turned to and read, seeking help from the Holy Spirit to understand it for my situation.

'When the unclean spirit has gone out of a person, it passes through waterless places seeking rest, and finding none it says, 'I will return to my house from which I came.' And when it comes, it finds the house swept and put in order. Then it goes and brings seven other spirits more evil than itself, and they enter and dwell there. And the last state of that person is worse than the first.'
(Luke 11:24-26 ESV)

I did not want the next stage in my life to be worse than the last, and I really wasn't understanding how this Scripture was helping. What would be the point in having all of this revelation and taking back the ground from the enemy only to find myself in a worse position than before? I believe that what happened next gave me the opportunity to visualise the situation and understand what I needed to prevent this catastrophe from occurring.

Imagine a house which is so dirty and so neglected that it would take a miracle to restore it to its former glory. Most would think it was too much effort, but someone special comes along and can visualise the finished product: a home so beautiful that it is fit for a King to live in. So he painstakingly washes and sweeps, paints and repairs and, as the time passes, this dilapidated shack turns into an exquisite place to live. Unfortunately, all of this activity has attracted the attention of the local villains, who are so jealous of this house that their desire to have it sends them into a frenzy of plotting, scheming and lying to acquire it unlawfully. They plan to take the house when it is empty and, under the cloak of darkness; legally occupy it under squatters' rights. The more villains there are, the harder it will be for the owner to evict them.

The owner has a detailed knowledge of the law and also understands what is going on in the wicked hearts of those who seek to steal the property. So, anticipating the jealousy of the villains, he figures out that if he leaves the house unattended for even one second the squatters will move in. By the time he is able to have the squatters removed, the house will again be destroyed. He understands that, if squatters gain entry to his property, it will be a tough job to have them removed. Predicting the outcome of making such a terrible mistake as leaving the property empty for any length of time, the owner moves in his new tenant immediately and makes sure that the house is occupied at all times.

I had been totally damaged, I thought, beyond repair; but that night, during the eight hours that I had talked with God, I had been washed, cleansed and restored. I was ready to be occupied by the new owner, and the Scripture is warning me of the dangers of leaving myself open to be occupied by the illegal tenants. I imagined my mind as the new house, restored and ready for occupancy. But there was something wrong with this picture: the house seemed dark and empty. I remember asking God, 'Why is my house still empty?

'Do you not know that you are God's temple and
that God's Spirit dwells in you?'
(1Corinthians 3:16 ESV)

God clearly replied here 'Because it hasn't been filled with my spirit'. My house had been filled with lies that were clogging up the ventilation. Scenes from past mistakes covered the windows, blocking the view to the world outside of my depression, obscuring the sun from shining through and leaving my house in darkness. It was a house that was hard to breathe in. Instantly, in this picture of the house, the lights came on and the house looked lived in. I knew from this point onwards that the light would occupy every corner and there was no room for darkness. The Holy Spirit was the owner/occupier. I had no idea that the Father had provided all that I needed: the Son for my Salvation and the Holy Spirit as my helper. My problem had been that I had never truly believed that God had provided everything that I needed. I believed that I was the only one that I could depend on. Nor had I ever truly surrendered my life to Him.

I had been holding back, living half of a life. I had been prepared to settle for a life with a disability, instead of surrendering my whole life to God. Although the disability was not a noticeable one to those around me, it was indeed a debilitating one. I felt immediately that the insanity that had kept me bent over and crippled for years had been removed. Suddenly, I was seeing straight ahead instead of looking to the floor. The spirit of infirmity that had gripped my mind was gone and I was able to look into the eyes of my Lord and Saviour without shame, guilt or fear. Now I was free from madness and full of hope for my future.

There have been many times since that night in my life when that fear and darkness has tried to take hold again. Fear never misses a trick. So the question is 'If fear is holding a person hostage, how do you make it release the hostage?' For me, it is to remember that this house is 'Occupied by the Holy Spirit'. There is a sign in the front garden of this house with those words on it. It stands as a reminder to me and a 'keep-out' sign for the enemy. There are no vacancies and no rooms to rent. What I have is a full house. This picture of a home that is lived in by the Father, Son and Holy Spirit was a vision that would encourage me in times that seem bleak - a milestone or landmark that I could return to as a reminder that would stop me from ever returning to that place of darkness. If fear or despair ever tried to grab hold of me, I would remember the house which is filled with light; and the thoughts would leave instantly.

The story in Luke about the unclean spirits helped me to see that all of my attempts to sweep them out - by listening to noise or taking pills to get it all under control, were futile. Only the full occupancy of the Holy Spirit would evict the enemy's deception. God is not the god of confusion, He gives us a clear mind; and, with the help of the Holy Spirit, I would sustain a healthy mind for many years to come.

Chapter 7
Be Careful What Influences You

'Dear friend, listen well to my words;
tune your ears to my voice.
Keep my message in plain view at all times.
Concentrate! Learn it by heart!
Those who discover these words live, really live;
body and soul, they're bursting with health.'
(Proverbs 4:20-22 The Message)

I hadn't tuned my ear to God's voice for such a long time. My concentration had been on my tales of woe and pity parties that had gone on for days, weeks and, in some cases, years. The voices I had entertained had helped me to stay in a place of bitterness and unforgiveness, and the voice of hope and truth I had ignored, based on the notion that it wasn't real. The only reality that I was experiencing was negativity and it had led to a downward spiral. That downward spiral was what had caused me to believe that my marriage was over.

I had looked forward to my 40th birthday for so long. It was going to be my turning point, that moment in time that I did something for me. My youngest child was thirteen and my oldest was twenty-one. I had been married to the most amazing man for eighteen years, and I wanted to mark my 40th birthday by doing something special. If I was more of an adrenaline junkie I would have climbed a mountain, maybe tried a bungie jump or even sky-diving, although why on earth anyone would want to jump out of a plane that is in perfect working order, I will never know! Whatever I did, I wanted to enjoy the day even if it was just spending it with friends and family. Mark knew this, he had known for a long time that I wanted to mark the occasion, but, as the time approached, we found that our financial situation meant that whatever we did would have to be low key. The previous week, Mark had asked me if had I decided what I wanted to do. Knowing we had very little money I casually said, 'Its ok, I don't want a fuss, surprise me.' And surprise me he did! Mark taking me at my word did nothing. My 40th birthday passed without event or even cake and I was devastated. Now, when your wife says she doesn't want a fuss, after planning to do something exciting for her birthday for a long time, I can guarantee that she does not mean it. I just want to repeat for all those gentlemen out there who are reading this, "think twice before deciding not to make a fuss". How could he have listened to my ramblings for the past year about a party or a holiday or a bungie jump and not realise that I wanted him to surprise me? This started the downward spiral. He obviously didn't care enough. I obviously meant nothing to him. He certainly didn't love me the way I loved him. Two years previous, when he turned 40, we went to America on holiday and I bought him a beautiful watch. He was not prepared; I had been. There was only one conclusion: he didn't love me.

This state of mind was an adventure playground that the enemy took advantage of and I was absolutely entitled to my hurt and anger. I never would have allowed Mark to feel so horrible at a time when good memories should have been made. Bitterness really took control, and I made sure at every opportunity that he never forgot how miserable I was feeling. I would repeat this story to anyone who would listen, as some of my friends reading this will remember. I was totally outraged and I made sure that everyone knew. In a bid to repair some of the damage, the following Christmas Mark attempted to give me a gift that had some meaning. I had wanted to learn how to ballroom dance and so he had paid for some lessons so that we could try to patch up this mess by doing something together. I, on the other hand, was done with gifts because I would not be taking these lessons, nor would I ever accept a gift from him or give him a gift. What would be the point? We had been living a lie. I loved him and he tolerated me for the sake of the kids; and when they were all eighteen and over, I would be out. This continued for two more years with the help of the whispers of the enemy. Those whispers came in the form of my own bad attitude and sense of entitlement and friends who helpfully took my side by feeding my paranoia and agreeing with my rantings. I made my own life miserable as well as Mark's and the kids', all because I refused to accept that Mark was not a mind reader and that there was a possibility that he really had genuinely misunderstood that what I say is not what I mean. This game that women play, where we hint at what we really mean and hope that the man is smart enough to read between the lines, really does only one thing: it sets them up to fail. Newsflash! They are not smart enough to understand your kind of crazy; *you* don't even understand your kind of crazy. Two years of our married life was stolen by this madness, when the memories of those two years could have been so different if I had said what I meant, or when Mark had apologised for getting it wrong, I had forgiven him instead of allowing the bitterness to control me. I am sure you have experienced the bitterness and hurt or anger that I am talking about. I found that I wasn't really aware of how these feelings could generate a force so powerful that it destroys every relationship in its path. It was subtle at first and then, when it gained strength, bitterness became the dominant emotion in my life. It really doesn't take much for the enemy to become a collaborator. He will keep you company and even become your best friend.

In the world without God, when I turned my back on the Christian life because I knew better, I had become my own worst enemy. In all of those dark, miserable years of my depression I hadn't asked nor had I heard what God was saying. I hadn't read my instruction book, nor had I talked to God about any of the nightmare I had been living, as I destroyed my marriage bit by bit in a frenzy of bitterness. I remember one of my daughters telling me that the Bible meant: **B**asic
                 Instruction
                 Before
                 Leaving
                 Earth.

This, I thought was a clever way to describe how important the Bible was to a child. Now I appreciate the simplicity of this statement and also just how significant it would be to this adult. Memories of times gone by and recollections of stories and sermons that I heard and had thought were gone for good, meant that I had a resource inside that I was able to access. Mostly I remembered the words I had read in the Bible, which until that night had been gathering a thick layer of dust, as I attempted to sort out my own life. Proverbs tells us to pay attention and learn the Word by heart that it may bring life. The chunks of the Bible that I had known had certainly brought me life that night, and I wanted so much to have more insight, more knowledge of God. I knew that to maintain a body, mind and soul so that they are bursting with health, I would need to put in what I wanted to get out. I had neglected the Word of God for so long and it had contained the nourishment that I had needed to gain abundant life, rather than the miserable existence I had accepted.

I was certainly paying attention now to what God was communicating to me, and I was grasping the full extent of who my enemy was. Although there is the physical and the spiritual side to depression that we mentioned earlier, there was also me. I know even when I said 'spiritual enemy' in chapter two, some of you were thinking, 'she is crazy'. You may even have thought there is no reason to read on, she is just another nut job who wants to blame her bad behaviour on 'the devil made me do it'. And I would not have blamed you, but you did keep reading, and now I ask you to please bear with me and I will try to explain why I am my own worst enemy.

The devil doesn't need to do a lot of work to gain a foothold in our lives; we see that in the example of my birthday mishap. That story is one of many that shows that there are times when we *The devil doesn't need a lot to get started* can do his work for him. It only takes a thought or a picture, or even the smallest piece of gossip, to influence your mind so dramatically that you form a bond with it and cherish it until it becomes part of you. You allow it to grow and then it becomes like a tumour that will eventually make your mind sick. If not instantly, somewhere down the line when you least expect it, the influence which was lurking in the shadows for years will suddenly take hold. So I ask myself, what had I been putting into this body? (let's not go there) Lets look at what I had been putting into this mind.

I was never careful about what I put into this very fragile mind of mine, and what I had classed as entertainment had sown the seeds of disbelief in the real battles that take place in the spiritual world. I loved to read books, any books, I just loved them, but, with time, Enid Blyton and the greats like Charles Dickens and C.S. Lewis were replaced by Stephen King and James Herbert. Then came the greatest invention ever for those who were too lazy to read: the video recorder.

'The Exorcist' and 'Zombies the Flesh-Eaters' were big blockbusters in my day. When we were kids, renting a video at the weekend was a really new concept, and my sister and I would take it in turns to choose. When it was my turn, it was always a horror. Freddie Kruger was the stuff of nightmares, but I loved it. Sitting on the edge of my seat, and not sure what was going to happen next, had been my idea of great entertainment right up into my twenties. Then I met my husband, Mark and it really wasn't his thing, so I found that I watched less and less of this genre and really got into my second passion which was space. I became quite the 'Trekkie', much to the embarrassment of my children, but that is a story for another day. Eventually I stopped watching the horrors altogether, but what the entertainment industry had done was make a nonsense of evil. The audience was desensitised to the idea of a real evil with the spinning heads, projectile vomit and the tomato sauce. In the horror movies the chapel or church building was a place of sanctuary where someone could run to in the event of being chased by the devil. It became the place of protection here, but in real life, quite clearly we see that the enemy can exist and attack anywhere. I can vouch for that. No

Trekkie: an avid fan of Star Trek and space travel

building or magic charm or holy water or garlic or silver can repel the influence of evil; nothing but the authority of Jesus can drive back the darkness of the enemy. I had fooled myself into believing that it was just a way to make money and thrill the audience using fear. In reality there were no demons and no devil; and, with regard to the celebration of Halloween, wasn't that just a money-making scheme generated by Hollywood? Evil even became glamourous as the devil was portrayed by exceptionally handsome men or scantily-clad actresses and the devil had become sexy. The public had accepted that evil is fantasy and, logically, what they don't believe in, can't harm them.

As a Christian, I had come to believe in a Spiritual realm, but I only really focused on the good stuff. The only supernatural that I wanted to encounter was the Holy Spirit. I didn't like the idea of demons and evil spirits because I remembered the fear that I used to get my kicks from. I could cope with the movies, but if it was real then the fear was real, and I had heard other Christians talk about the devil, some of them to the extreme. Maybe you have met them too; the only thing they want to talk about are demons and they see them everywhere on the ceiling, in the corners, when they stir in the milk into their coffee and in the cream bun that just spoke to them and said eat me. I had seen a Van Helsing movie and I didn't fancy hunting demons at the weekend. I was a Christian who attended church twice a week not Buffy the Vampire Slayer.

I wanted to talk about Jesus, the lovely man who made a way for me to get into heaven and who was gentle Jesus meek and mild, with gorgeous blue eyes like Robert Powell in the Jesus of Nazareth movie. I didn't want to be one of those crazy people who knew more about the devil than their Saviour; to me, that was insane. So, I thought if I ignored all that stuff then it wouldn't affect me. If I decided not get involved in these issues, then I would not have any problems at all. The pastors and ministers could handle all that spiritual stuff, I was just your everyday church-goer. Ignorance is bliss, as the saying goes.

If only I had understood that this melting pot of junk that I put into my mind could influence me in ways that I never could have imagined. Make sure that your worst enemy is not what is living between your ears. I needed to stop putting rubbish into my mind that would take me down a road I did not want to be on. In my case it was horror, but think of all the other things that we accept as entertainment. Sex, violence and bad language are all used now to make a TV programme more authentic. The virtual world of video games has allowed our young men to become gangsters, pimps and car thieves, snipers and bombers, and all in the name of entertainment. Our young women think it is ok to read "Fifty Shades of

Grey" and go in droves to the cinema to watch the screenplay, hoping that Jamie Dornan will have his clothes off in most of the movie. It is all about the eye candy, and all of it is used by the enemy to keep their minds clogged up with junk. Rant over!

> *'Be sober-minded; be watchful. Your adversary the devil prowls around like a roaring lion, seeking someone to devour.'*
> *(1 Peter 5:8 ESV)*

Consider the things that we put into our minds on a daily basis because we have become immune to the effects of the language or imagery that is used. We are no longer offended by nudity or sexual acts that leave nothing to the imagination. We are not shocked by violence that is inflicted on one person by another in the name of entertainment; and true evil is the stuff of superstitious fairy tales and horror movies designed to frighten little children into believing there is a bogeyman under the bed. If, however, we are cautious and careful and clear-minded, just as we are instructed in Peter, then we will never forget that the enemy is prowling at the door like a lion waiting to pounce. I heard this phrase used in a sermon recently, 'evil thoughts can inspire the demonic'. What if what

"The greatest trick the devil ever pulled was convincing the world he did not exist" Charles Baudelaire

we put into our minds inspires the enemy to pounce in our ignorant state? Then we really are our own worst enemy. The mind is a greenhouse of opportunity for the enemy to cultivate his own agenda; and, if we are not careful, we can and do help him by planting the seeds for him.

This world is ruled by the enemy of God, and so the things of this world that are not of God are influencing us in ways that we cannot understand or control. But will we listen? Some will, others won't, but we are told this in 2 Corinthians 4:4,

> *'In their case the god of this world has blinded the minds of the unbelievers, to keep them from seeing the light of the gospel of the glory of Christ, who is the image of God.'*
> *(2 Corinthians 4:4 ESV)*

I didn't want to be blinded like the mind of the unbeliever, and I had been for so long. The time had come to change everything and replace the junk with the truth of the Word of God.

> *'Whoever walks with the wise becomes wise, but the companion of fools suffers harm.'*
> *(Proverbs 13:1 NRS)*

Proverbs warns us about the company we keep. As most of my friends were from the church, it seemed to me that it was impossible for me to be keeping the wrong company. How wrong I was.

I had become a moaner - never satisfied, always complaining, argumentative and always right. When I was in church on Sunday, I did not discuss the things of God over coffee after the service. I did not even discuss the sermon of that day, just the things that I had an opinion on, like what I had watched on TV that week or maybe the news or even the weather, and we have certainly plenty to complain about in that department in this country as it never stops raining. I discussed the state of the education system in this country and engaged in many discussions about food as that was my job at the time. But my conversations never started with. 'I was reading my Bible the other day... 'or' that point that the pastor made in the service really made me think about my relationship with God'. It was as though I had come to church, sat through the service and got it over with and now I would occupy the next twenty minutes with some small-talk before getting on with my life. My conversations were shallow, when I had them, and even then I had probably made the conscious choice to leave church as quickly as possible so as to not engage with people.

Then there were others like me who were also depressed; I kept company with them. Birds of a feather flock together. But none of us was wise enough to see that we fed each other's paranoia. Discussing which anti-depressants were stronger or which one would have helped you sleep was not the way of wise counsel. There were plenty of others with strong opinions like myself and we soon made friends, putting the whole world to rights at every opportunity, no matter whose character was assassinated (usually Mark's for messing up my birthday). In those conversations we left no trace of integrity in any one of us; neither those speaking nor those listening knew what integrity was. Everyone has an opinion about how they can do things better, and I never kept my opinion to myself. I wanted to and needed to walk with the wise. Finding myself a self-help group of other Christians' in the same situation as myself was not the wisest move I had ever made. I knew it, and they knew it, but there was such a force drawing us together that we almost couldn't help ourselves. Tragedies and dramas, horrific experiences and gossip are all things that, when constantly regurgitated, kept me in emotional turmoil and tormented anger, and so it went on and on. There was nothing encouraging or uplifting about those conversations. That is until one day someone new came along and the group, being helpful and friendly welcomed the new person. As soon as was reasonably possible, I would emotionally dump my stuff all over them too, if they would listen, continuing the cycle of destruction. I told the same stories that dredged up my entitlement to be angry, keeping me in a never-ending circle of irritation and anguish. What started off as a couple of like-minded people became a coven of demented witches who sympathised with each other. There were even some guys who had gotten in on the act over the years too; gossip and bad behavior is not exclusive to the females of the church.

I needed to find people who were good Godly company, who knew the Word of God and were not afraid to use it as a way to guide and teach. I don't mean the well-meaning scripture-slinging cowboy who has a wee verse for every occasion that he shoots from the hip to make you feel worse about your sinful nature. I mean the person who wants to help you, pray with you and mentor you, so you can grow spiritually and leave behind unholy behavior.

I had allowed outside influences to steal my peace, joy, love and hope, and in turn I had also been the damaging influence in the lives of others by stealing their peace, joy, love and hope even, if I did it unintentionally. Let's be clear about the word 'unintentionally' that I used in the last sentence. I chose to regurgitate my rubbish on a regular basis, so it was not an accident that the sad by-product of this was the harm that I caused my friends, and I should have known better.

*'It only takes a spark, remember, to set off a forest
fire. A careless or wrongly placed word out of your
mouth can do that. By our speech we can ruin the
world, turn harmony to chaos, throw mud on a
reputation, send the whole world up in smoke and
go up in smoke with it, smoke right from
the pit of hell.'*
(James 3:5-6 the Message)

Things needed to change, I needed to change, and the
only way to change was to be careful what I said and
what I listened to. Choosing carefully the company I
kept was one of the most uncomfortable things I ever
had to do. There were people that I classed as good
friends, but I was not helping them, nor they me,
and so for a short time I needed to keep my distance
until I learned how to behave in a Godly manner. If I
found myself in conversations that would cause harm
to anyone, should it be those listening or speaking,
I would remove myself from those situations until
I was able to ask boldly, 'What does the Bible say
about this?' I did this not because I had a holier-than-
thou attitude, but so that I could be an encourager
and maybe one day be one of the wise whom others
would enjoy keeping company with.

And finally the TV. There was only one rule that
applied here (and still does): never watch something
that I would turn off if Jesus was in the room. I
explained earlier that God is ever present, so this

really applies to every part of my life, and I will ask you all as Christians the same question. Would you be in that bar drinking that cocktail or having that conversation or even looking at porn on the computer (yes Christians get caught in this too) if you could physically see God in the room with you? Be careful of the foothold you give to the enemy; the last thing you want to do is give him a helping hand.

Chapter 8
Today's Hunger for God

*'I have been crucified with Christ. It is no longer
I who live, but Christ who lives in me. And the life
I now live in the flesh I live by faith in the Son of
God, who loved me and gave himself for me.'*
(Galatians 2:20 ESV)

A new life awaited me and I couldn't wait for morning! You see, I hadn't realised the time and by now Mark had already come to bed and was asleep beside me. By the time God and I had finished our conversation that night, I knew that change was coming and it was going to be amazing. It was now the early hours of the morning and the room and everything about me, even the deep breathing of my husband beside me, was so peaceful. I felt the excitement of the new hope that I had to look forward to and, as I closed my Bible I knew that tomorrow was bringing a new life that God had for me. The voices were silent and, as I sat in the presence of God, I knew that His work was done and that I needed to go to sleep. The lamp was on Mark's side of the bed, so I got up and walked around to turn it off. Walking back to my side in the dark, a voice spoke and said, 'what's under the bed?' Again fear gripped me for just a second. I know that sounds childish, but fear of the dark can grip anyone, young or old, if it is allowed to take hold. I found, my answer came with such conviction that I surprised myself by speaking out loud. I replied, 'What's under the bed? Nothing. Fear, you are a weapon of the enemy and you have no authority here. Go back to where you came from for I am a child of God and I am going to sleep.'

> *'Behold, I have given you authority to tread on serpents and scorpions, and over all the power of the enemy, and nothing shall hurt you. Nevertheless, do not rejoice in this, that the spirits are subject to you, but rejoice that your names are written in heaven.'*
> *(Luke 10:19-20 ESV)*

The anxiety that I had felt left instantly and, without the aid of sleeping tablets or headphones with the sounds of the sea to sooth me, I went to sleep. For the first time in a very long time, I was at peace and I had a great night's sleep.

The next morning, I got to share everything that God had shown me with Mark. Although he probably was unsure if this was another one of my extreme highs, he listened and we talked for the first time in a long time. I was able to look at him without bitterness oozing out from my pores. He watched me closely over the next few weeks as things began to change. I think that he knew that God had done something special that night for all of us, but he was cautious as he dared to hope that it would last. My mood stayed positive and I spent a lot of time apologising for my behaviour. After a while there would be other challenges for Mark and me, but we now placed God in the centre; and, as we both carved a life with purpose for Him, we worked on our problems together with God right there in the middle.

*'And though a man might prevail against one who is
alone, two will withstand him-- a threefold
cord is not quickly broken.'
(Ecclesiastes 4:12 ESV)*

I am a visual person, so now when I think about our marriage I see us like the picture in Ecclesiastes, Mark and I, brought together in a strong rope by the third strand, which is God. Without God in our marriage there would be no strength, and eventually the two strands would unravel and fall apart. Forgiveness played a major role in this process, and we are now stronger than ever as a couple. What seemed hopeless, and was bound for the divorce courts, has been repaired and restored to a place of love beyond anything either of us could have patched together from the wreckage. God is good.

My kids are awesome; they carried on as normal. Now in their twenties, they get embarrassed by my stories, but only because they didn't see things the way I did. For them, there were times when things looked a bit odd, but most of the madness was contained in my head; and my regrets, well they are mine to deal with. I love my kids with all my heart, and I am so proud of each of them as they have moved into their own adventures of adult life. I think that their biggest worry had been that a divorce was on the cards, due to all the fighting that had gone on, but now they know that there is no chance of Mark and me splitting up.

When we get the opportunity, we remind them that it is God's promises that keep us together. Our hope is that they, too, will find that God-strength in their own marriages and relationships as it really is too hard to find answers without Him. The worst they have to face with Mark and me is the fact that they are totally grossed out by the holding hands of their middle-aged parents, so we try to keep it to a minimum.

You see, knowing my enemy gave me confidence to understand the lies and fear that he wants me to live in. However, this was not the most important lesson that I had learned that night. The most important thing for me was knowing my Father. I was not alone and I was not crazy as the enemy would lead me to believe. Jesus speaks of the prodigal son, and we all know the story, but I want to show you something that captured me about this story,

> *'And he arose and came to his father. But while he*
> *was still a long way off, his father saw him and*
> *felt compassion, and ran and embraced him*
> *and kissed him.'*
> *(Luke 15:20 ESV)*

The father didn't wait until the son reached him; he ran toward the son in this story, just as my heavenly Father ran towards me. He had stopped me in my tracks and had spent the whole night embracing me with His words, assurances and promises. These had all been placed in His word and in my memory for such a time as this. The most powerful weapon in the world is the Word of God. In it is every truth that I need to keep my sanity. There is promise after promise; it really is the instruction manual for everything life throws at us. If we want to know more about God, we will find the information we need in the Scriptures. The accounts of the life, death and resurrection of Jesus are found there. The information we need to be reconciled to the Father are right there in the pages of the Bible. To neglect it in the way that I had was one of the many reasons I had found myself in a place of torment. Now when I read, I do it with the understanding that it may be difficult to grasp the meanings sometimes, but I know that the Holy Spirit will guide me as I become more familiar with the writings in it. One thing I do know is that I cannot live this life with second-hand knowledge of the Bible; I must read it for myself and learn to understand it for myself. If I don't open it I won't automatically know what is inside just because I carry it to church on a Sunday. I had tried that for years, I can promise you it doesn't work.

I have found that I have become hungry for the things of God. I had heard others talk like this, but I had never really understood what they meant. I will try to explain this new phenomenon to the best of my ability.

"As a deer pants for the water
so my soul longs after you,
you alone are my heart's desire,
and I long to worship you"
Martin J Nystrom

I sang this song many times in my youth and now I understand that it is not just a nice idea from the Psalmist, it is a true desire of my heart. I had filled my life with junk, but the time that I had spent with God that night had almost felt like a detox. I looked up this word, as we hear it a lot in this wonderful world of fads and diets. In the context of that night, I think the definition is very appropriate: *to abstain from or rid the body of toxic or unhealthy substances.* I had definitely experienced a mental detox and I felt great. My mind had been left clear from the madness, and the freedom I was now experiencing was nothing short of miraculous. But I want to highlight what I think is the most important part of the definition which is *'abstain from'*. I needed to abstain from the influences that would clog my mind with junk. That's why I started to be careful about the company I kept and turned off the TV when something inappropriate came on. I tried not to engage in wrongful conversation; and, when I started down a road of wrong thought and negative imaginations, I was honest about it to myself, to Mark and to God. Recognising those things didn't always come naturally, so I started to seek Godly counsel. When I found that my behaviour did not come up to scratch, I had given permission to those whom I trusted to guide me back to the right path. I was hungry for the things of God and so I searched the scriptures to get to know Him; and the more time I spent with Him, the hungrier I got for the things of God.

The only thing that I can compare this desire to is when I first met Mark. He was handsome, funny, charming and good fun to be with. As I spent more time with him I began to love everything about him. I missed him when he wasn't with me and I found that I thought about him all the time. I couldn't wait for the next time that I would be in his company. Once we were married, our whole lives revolved around each other, and it never occurred to me that we would ever not be together. Of course, when I started to listen to the enemy, those little things that I had found so charming became the irritations that caused estrangement. Doesn't it say in Song of Solomon 2:15 that it is the little foxes that spoil the vines, it really is the little things that spoil the precious gift of marriage. Once that junk and rubbish (or little foxes) were removed, I again experienced the unity brought by the unblemished desire to be together. That hunger and longing also applies to my relationship with God.

If it is not Godly, I have no interest in it. The only influence that I am interested in is God - in my home, in my relationships, in my work-place and in every aspect of my life. In the eighties, we wore T-shirts which said "Choose Life" and that is exactly what I am doing. Wanting the things of God is no bad thing and so I would challenge anyone who has found their life spiralling out of control to stop and seek God for the answers. For the Bible says,

'Ask, and it will be given to you; seek, and you will find; knock, and it will be opened to you. For everyone who asks receives, and the one who seeks finds, and to the one who knocks it will be opened.'
(Matthew 7:7-8 ESV)

As for me and the condition of my body, mind and spirit today, the song that comes from Psalm 42 expresses not only my present state of mind but also my future and purpose. Martin J Nystrom describes perfectly my hunger for God today in his beautiful song, 'As the deer'. I will leave you with the first verse and chorus as a taster to the depths to which a desire for a relationship with God can go.

As The Deer

As the deer pants for the water
So my soul longs after you
You alone are my heart's desire
And I long to worship you

You alone are my strength, my shield
To You alone may my spirit yield
You alone are my heart's desire
And I long to worship you

by Martin Nystrom

Chapter 9
I Have No More To Give You

"To have and to hold from this day forward......"

You are probably wondering when I am going to get around to explaining the ring on the front cover. It is a copy of one of the eleven gold rings found on the Girona, which was part of the Spanish Armada, shipwrecked off the County Antrim coast on 28th October 1588. The ring bears a sculpted hand holding a single heart, and a message in Spanish is engraved on the outside of the band. The inscription reads:

'No tengo mas que dar te'
('I have no more to give you.')

Some of the articles written about these rings claim that they were Spanish wedding rings. The bride and groom exchange the rings, symbolising each giving his/her heart to the other, as a token of their undying love. Isn't that a beautiful idea that, on your wedding day, you and your soon-to-be partner for life would exchange rings that express that you are giving them everything, holding back nothing, totally united on the day of your wedding and forever? Romantic, even detailed, but no different from the promises made when we exchange plain gold rings in our marriage ceremonies today. Does anyone in this day and age really understand the covenant that they are entering into on their wedding day? These days we see so little commitment from people that they don't even bother to get married. They live with each other for a while, maybe test the waters a bit, but if there is no marriage certificate then either one of them can walk away at any time without ever having really committed to the whole thing in the first place. Or they get married because they think it is a good idea at the time, but have a solicitor on speed-dial just in case.

I have come to understand that, as I had blundered my way through my Christian life, I had never really committed my all to God. I tested the waters a bit, maybe even took it seriously here and there and tried to make a bigger effort, but I had always held back. God was part of my life in as much as I would allow Him to be - a one-sided relationship which, I am sure, some of us can relate to at one time or another in our lives. I have, of course, been on the receiving end of a casual encounter, that I had hoped would lead to commitment, only to find that after a few short months the novelty had worn off. I remember the devastation of unrequited love and the thoughts that my broken heart would never be the same again. To my dismay, I began to see that I was the one dishing out that heartbreak in my lackadaisical attitude towards my relationship with God.

Thankfully that was not God's attitude toward me. In the same way we enter into a covenant or contract with our husbands or wives, God has entered into a covenant with us, those of us, of course, who are brave enough to make the commitment at all. These days the word 'covenant' is rarely used, the word 'contract' which is used to replace it is just not strong enough. In the culture we live in a very clever solicitor can get you out of a contract. Even if a contract seems airtight, you can always buy your way out of it. The old phrase 'everyone has a price' comes into play here. A covenant, on the other hand, has no expiry date, it has no opt-out clauses and the parties involved are bound by the conditions of the covenant until death. God has made a covenant with me and it begins with;

"For God so loved the world, that He gave His only Son, that whoever believes in Him should not perish but have eternal life."
(John 3:16 ESV)

God had sent His son to die so that, if I believe, I will have eternal life. That hardly seems fair. God's side of the bargain means that Jesus, His Only Son, dies so that I can gain eternal life. Simply stated, God has sent his Son to die in my place. So, all I need to do to receive eternal life is believe or trust in this act of substitution. It was my sin that separated me from God and, as the offering of Jesus on the cross wiped the slate clean, I could begin again, free from the guilt and shame of the life I had lived and it would cost me nothing. God gave His Son for me to be able to spend eternity in His presence. Under normal circumstances, this seems like a one-sided contract and the thought would cross my mind that there was a catch. What was my part to play in this covenant?

"The time is fulfilled, and the kingdom of God is at
hand; repent and believe in the gospel."
(Mark 1:15 ESV)

That was it, all I had to do was repent and believe in the Lord Jesus Christ. I didn't have to sacrifice anything, but God sacrificed His Son to make this covenant with me, and there is no catch.

"Trust in the LORD with all your heart, and do
not rely on your own understanding. Acknowledge
him in all your ways, and he will make your
paths straight."
(Proverbs 3:5 NET)

To be able to live under this promise all I had to do was repent and believe, that was it, because God had already done it all - no catch and no small print. Looking back at how I had been living, it looked like I had refused God's love. Thankfully, He did not give up on me. Not once had He left me to fend for myself. I had never faced this life by myself. The thing is that the promise to make my paths straight wasn't just intended for me. In the Old Testament, when Moses speaks to the Israelites about crossing over the Jordan into the promised land, he reminds them of God's promise,

*"Be strong and courageous. Do not fear or be
in dread of them, for it is the LORD your God
who goes with you. He will not leave you or
forsake you."*
(Deuteronomy 31:6 ESV)

When David speaks to Solomon about the completion
of the temple, he reminds him of God's promise,

*"Then David said to Solomon his son, "Be strong
and courageous and do it. Do not be afraid and do
not be dismayed, for the LORD God, even my God,
is with you. He will not leave you or forsake you,
until all the work for the service of the house of
the LORD is finished."*
(1Chronicles 28:20 ESV)

In Matthew's Gospel, when the disciples were
instructed by Jesus to go and make disciples of the
nations and baptise them, He said,

*".... and behold, I am with you always, to the end of
the age."*
(Matthew 28:20 ESV)

Paul, when he writes to the church in Philippi,
reminds them,

131

> *"do not be anxious about anything, but in*
> *everything by prayer and supplication with*
> *thanksgiving let your requests be made known to*
> *God. And the peace of God, which surpasses all*
> *understanding, will guard your hearts and your*
> *minds in Christ Jesus."*
> *(Philippians 4:6-7 ESV)*

When I would not listen to God, I believe He found ways to get through to me, even to the point where I was actually given the ring shown on the front cover as a reminder of His love for me. A friend from church had handed me a card one Sunday morning when I was right in the thick of a particularly dark bout of depression. There have been other times when people have come to encourage me with a note or a word of reassurance that God is with me. This time my friend had a story to tell. She had been in a charity shop probably about fifteen years previously, when she came across this ring and bought it. She had never worn it and so she thought that she would give it away. She kept it in a jewellry box for years wondering who she would give it to. As time passed she had completely forgotten about the ring until she had come across it that week and felt that the time had come to give it away. She believed that this ring was for me, to encourage me to remember that God had given me everything I needed to endure the hard times that life could bring. In a little purple bag was the ring and on the card was a description of where the rings were found and the meaning of the engraved words on the ring. I put it on and have not removed it since. This little ring is a constant reminder of the amazing promise that God has given me everything. You see, God's promise to me was binding, never to be broken.

In the not so distant future, that little ring would be the reminder I needed that God had given me everything to withstand the storms that life can bring. There have, of course, been many times when I have felt shipwrecked. When I look at the ring, I have the visual reminder right there with me of the promise from God that He has in fact equipped me for every eventuality. Just like the wedding ring that Mark gave me on my wedding day, my Spanish ring is a ring of promise. It has no magic powers, nor is it a good luck charm, it is just a reminder of the promise of God never to leave me nor forsake me.

*'For we all have become like one who is
[ceremonially] unclean [like a leper],
And all our deeds of righteousness are like
filthy rags;
We all wither and decay like a leaf,
And our wickedness [our sin, our injustice, our
wrongdoing], like the wind, takes us away [carrying
us far from God's favor, toward destruction].'
(Isaiah 64:6 AMP)*

I had been at the point of total bankruptcy as my body, mind and spirit had given up. I had nothing left absolutely nothing. I was broken and in serious need of repair. I had nothing left to try to bargain with God.

Even as believers our good works are still filthy rags, reminding us everyday that it's about His grace not our best efforts. Have you ever made a desperate cry? You know the one that goes, 'oh God if you will just get me out of this mess I will go to church for the rest of my life.' I have, many times. I didn't even have the will to try to bargain with God or to try to gain His favour. By the time the depression had control of me, I had lost the will to live. Can you imagine how one-sided the marriage or covenant between me and God would be? I can just hear those vows - mine would sound like this:

'I, Anna, take you, God, to be my lawfully-wedded husband, my constant friend, my faithful partner and my love from this day forward. I have nothing more to give you, everything in me is broken, battered and bruised, but if you are happy with this mess then here I am.'

And he accepts. God's vows would be so different:

'I, God, take you, Anna, to be my lawfully-wedded wife and my love from this day forward. I offer you my solemn vow to be your faithful partner in sickness and in health, in good times and in bad, and in joy as well as in sorrow. I promise to love you unconditionally, to laugh with you and cry with you, and to cherish you forever. I have given you everything.'

Now that is a promise and covenant worth entering into. Thankfully for me, that was all the commitment that God wanted from me. I can say, 'God, I have nothing more to give you.' I can hand over the tatters of my life and heart, and that is all that He will ask of me. This heart that has been broken, stepped on, battered and bruised by my attempts to live this life my way I can hand over to God, and it is all that He asks of me. It is with a confidence in God's love for me that I can now pray the words of the Psalmist below,

'Search me, O God, and know my heart! Try me and know my thoughts! And see if there be any grievous way in me, and lead me in the way everlasting!'
(Psalm 139:23-24 ESV)

God has given me everything and asks for nothing in return except my heart, no matter what condition it is in. There are no conditions to this union, nor are there any hoops to jump through or making-up to do. I just come as I am because He can change me.

135

He is the one constant in my life that never changes. Hebrews says this so well:

> *'God means what he says. What he says goes. His powerful Word is sharp as a surgeon's scalpel, cutting through everything, whether doubt or defence, laying us open to listen and obey. Nothing and no one is impervious to God's Word. We can't get away from it—no matter what.'*
> *(Hebrews 3:12-13 The Message)*

The whole idea of giving my life over to anyone is totally alien to a control freak like me. On the other hand, it is such a relief. With each passing day, I have received the promises of God and lived a life free from the torment of depression. God has kept His promises and I have found my strength in Him. Things have changed and I have changed as I now seek Him in every eventuality of my life. This is what the Bible says about this change;

> *"Whenever, though, they turn to face God as Moses did, God removes the veil and there they are—face-to-face! They suddenly recognize that God is a living, personal presence, not a piece of chiselled stone. And when God is personally present, a living Spirit, that old, constricting legislation is recognised as obsolete. We're free of it! All of us! Nothing between us and God, our faces shining with the brightness of his face. And so we*

are transfigured much like the Messiah, our lives
gradually becoming brighter and more beautiful as
God enters our lives and we become like him."
(2 Corinthians 3:16-18 Message)

This is how my future looks: a life-time and an eternity in the presence of God, reflecting His Glory in total freedom and giving Him the glory for the amazing work He has done in me. This is, of course, not an exclusive offer to me alone. Christian, if you are tormented and in the middle of a battle with depression, stay strong, and know without doubt the God you serve, for the Bible says;

Glory -
Magnificence
or Great

"The LORD is my strength and my
[impenetrable] shield;
My heart trusts [with unwavering confidence] in
Him, and I am helped;
Therefore my heart greatly rejoices,
And with my song I shall thank Him and praise
Him.
The LORD is their [unyielding] strength,
And He is the fortress of salvation to His anointed.
Save Your people and bless Your inheritance;
Be their shepherd also, and carry them forever."
(Psalm 28:7-9 Amp)

If you have been given this book in the hope that you will find the answer to your depression, and you have

137

never committed your life to the Lord, then I ask you to consider this your opportunity. It really is as simple as *repent and believe*. The answer to everything that life throws at us is Jesus. *Our sin nature leads to actions and thoughts that separates us from God.* God desires us to be restored in relationship with Him and so He sent His Son Jesus to die in our place, the just for the unjust, so that our sins could be forgiven. Because of the death and the resurrection of Jesus Christ, we can live this life as we were supposed to, in communion with Him. You don't have to change or sort yourself out to come to Jesus - He wants you just as you are. We can be born again, given a new nature, enabling us to live in communion with Him. It's all about grace, it is God who saves, it is God who forgives your sins, it is God who gives you a new nature. He enables you to pray this prayer:

Father, I come to you,
I have been living my life for myself,
I have done many things that would not please you,
but I am asking for forgiveness for my sins.
I need you in my life.
I believe that Jesus died on the cross and rose
again to save me.
I come to you now and ask you to take control of
my life.
I desire to live my life for you and I ask you all
these things in the name of Jesus Christ our Lord.
Amen

I Have No More to Give You

Chapter 10
Surround Yourself with the Things of God

*'The heavens declare the glory of God; the sky displays his handiwork. Day after day it speaks out; night after night it reveals his greatness.
There is no actual speech or word, nor is its voice literally heard. Yet its voice echoes throughout the earth; its words carry to the distant horizon.'*
(Psalm 19:1-4 NET)

I am ending this book in the same place where I started - in Browns Bay, the little beach not far from my home. Today the sun is shining (unusual for Northern Ireland, I know) and there is a cool breeze coming off the sea. Here I am, enjoying the warmth of the sand under my feet and the sun on my face. As I sit watching the waves roll in, I could be on any beach in the world right now, but this little inlet on the shores of County Antrim is by far the most beautiful for me. I am remembering the sounds that rescued me that day so long ago now, and I hear the ripple of the waves on the shore. I just love knowing that I am sitting right in the centre of the glory of God - this beach and everything around me is His creation. Even though the beach is full of families and there is nothing quiet about this place today, the squeals of delight as the children play make me smile. It is so beautiful here, and I am grateful for this moment in time for it is a gift that reminds me to surround myself with the things of God.

I would suggest to anyone who has found himself in the same position as I have, to surround himself with God's creation. Nature itself had such a calming influence on me that, as I sit once more on this beach, I am only now realising why the sounds of the sea soothed me enough so that I could sleep. God created it. Nothing man made ever really helped me. Listening now to the comforting movement of the waves and hearing the gentle rush of the breeze as it cools my face from the heat of the sun, I know, even though I didn't understand it at the time, that even in nature there was a solution to my madness.

Let me take you back a couple of years. The world says that depression is a reoccurring, condition and so I lived with this idea for a little while after that night. Somewhere, in the back of my mind, I believed that there was a possibility that there would be another episode of manic behaviour. That day came when I least expected it, about two years later. I woke up with a black cloud over my head. The thought that had enveloped me was the memory of a horrible fight Mark and I had had years earlier. It had wounded me quite deeply and I felt the hurt that came with the thought. The memory of what I had felt reared its ugly head and anger rose up. How dare he treat me that way! Who did he think he was! It was such a strong emotion that I really wanted to call him and fight with him over the phone. I tried to shake it off and so I jumped into the shower to start the morning and then the pity party started. I really felt sorry for myself and, the more I tried to shake off this feeling, the sadness and loneliness that I was experiencing at that time was like a heavy weight pressing down on me. As the tears ran down my face I made a feeble attempt to pray, but nothing was lifting this mood. I couldn't find the words. The next stage was total defeat. It was nice to have had a couple of years depression free. I wonder how long it will last this time? If I couldn't pray, then there was no chance of my day getting any better. It was like stepping back in time and, for what seemed like an eternity, I stood as the hot water ran over me, totally unaware of the presence of God which, believe me, was there. I had forgotten everything that I had learned and out of habit I began to sing. Yes, I admit it - I am a shower singer, a very loud one when there is no one else in the house. This time I wasn't really very enthusiastic, a little bit of a hum, slowly at first because I was having trouble remembering the words. Suddenly the latest worship song that we'd been singing in church came into my head so I began to sing it. I can't even remember now which one it was, but, as the words came back to me, within minutes the mood that had weighed so heavy began to lift and then I was able to pray. Before I knew it, the battle was won and I no longer felt overwhelmed but victorious.

Worship, I believe, has been a great weapon in my battle since that day in the shower. When I found myself in a place that was clearly going to lead me to despair, I would sing praise and worship songs and, without fail, I would find myself in a place of peace. That peace would then lead me into a place of conversation with my Father and again another battle to separate me from Him was prevented. I remembered reading about King Saul and how he would send for David to play his harp and sooth his troubled mind.

*'So whenever the spirit from God would come
upon Saul, David would take his lyre and play it.
This would bring relief to Saul and make him feel
better. Then the evil spirit would leave him alone.'
(1Samuel 16:23 NET)*

Paul and Silas are another example of the power of prayer and worship.

*'About midnight Paul and Silas were praying and
singing hymns to God, and the rest of the prisoners
were listening to them. Suddenly a great earthquake
occurred, so that the foundations of the prison were
shaken. Immediately all the doors flew open, and
the bonds of all the prisoners
came loose.'
(Acts 16:25-26 NET)*

Worship has been a mighty weapon against depression in this battle and many others that I have fought. It helped me to reconnect with God. Without it, who knows how long it would have taken me to shut down the negative thoughts that were ready to consume me that day in the shower. When I am separated from God I feel despondent and discouraged, but worship returns me to a place of peace and an awareness of His presence. Like Paul and Silas, I am freed from whatever traps me and keeps me in chains.
You are probably wondering how this story connects to me sitting on the beach. This was my thought.

The Scriptures tell us:

'For you shall go out in joy and be led forth in peace; the mountains and the hills before you shall break forth into singing, and all the trees of the field shall clap their hands.'
(Isaiah 55:12 ESV)

'when the morning stars sang in chorus, and all the sons of God shouted for joy'
(Job 38:7 NET)

"Make a joyful noise to the LORD, all the earth; break forth into joyous song and sing praises! Sing praises to the LORD with the lyre, with the lyre and the sound of melody! With trumpets and the sound of the horn make a joyful noise before the King, the LORD! Let the sea roar, and all that fills it; the world and those who dwell in it! Let the rivers clap their hands; let the hills sing for joy together before the LORD"
(Psalm 98:4-9 ESV)

Praise him, sun and moon, praise him, all you shining stars!
(Psalm 148:3 ESV)

In all of these verses I read how nature also worships God. I know that we don't literally hear nature sing but what soothed me that first day in Browns Bay was the roar of the sea praising its creator. Psalm 148 talks of all creation that praises God. Even in the New Testament, Jesus says that if the people ceased to praise then the rocks would cry out,

"Blessed is the King who comes in the name of the Lord! Peace in heaven and glory in the highest!" And some of the Pharisees in the crowd said to him, "Teacher, rebuke your disciples." He answered, "I tell you, if these were silent, the very stones would cry out."
(Luke 19:38-40 ESV)

Everyone worships differently - we see that in the variety of churches every Sunday. All creation worships God, every animal makes a different sound, and, just because we do not understand or sometimes even hear, it doesn't mean that it doesn't happen. So, is it too far-fetched to believe that the rhythmic sound of nature was the sea making a joyful noise before the King that day, as described in the Psalms? Is it too much to believe that I was able to engage with the glory of nature in order to connect with the peace of God? I found rest that day through the sound of God's creation, so isn't it possible that God really has given me everything that I need to truly have victory in every battle? I am surrounded by the glory of His creation. Surely this could be another way to engage in the presence of God.

What is worship? More importantly, who is the object of our worship? We are all worshippers and worshipping is to glorify and commend what we cherish. The object of our affection is God, so, as we turn away from the things that we idolise, we turn towards to God whom we love. The Bible says that God is a jealous God and the Spirit yearns jealously for our undivided adoration. I had become so self-absorbed that I wasn't paying Him any attention. All my thoughts were focused on myself. I needed to look away from myself and fix my eyes on Him.

As I am sure you have realised by now, the enemy never gives up; he may get knocked back, but he never gives up. John Stott says:

> *"If the devil can't lure us to do evil he is content to occupy our minds with things that don't matter."*

That was the old me, the one who did everything to be a good person but had a mind that was occupied with issues that were so massive that the whole sky was falling in. A lot of those issues, as Stott says, don't matter.

> *"For if you forgive others their trespasses, your heavenly Father will also forgive you. But if you do not forgive others their trespasses, neither will your Father forgive your trespasses."*
> *(Matthew 6: 14-15 ESV)*

Unforgiveness played a big part of my thought process and now, even though it isn't always easy, I will forgive even if the person isn't sorry. This I do for my sake and no one else's. I will not allow unforgiveness to poison my mind or steal my peace, because the only one who is robbed of peace is me. Unforgiveness only affects the person who is holding tight to it. Let's be honest, the other party is probably getting on with their life. If, on the other hand, the other party is seeking forgiveness, then peace is restored in both camps. We have then a win-win situation, and the enemy loses again.

I am not saying that the battle against depression is easy, but I have found victory in God. Since that amazing night in 2012, I have had many trials and faced many battles, but I have never attempted to face them alone. God has placed me in a great church and given me amazing friends. He has completely restored and healed my family and my marriage. He has given me a purpose and a calling, and I know with all my heart that I will serve Him until the end of my days.

This new-found hope that I have is due to His grace and the peace that it brings as I trust in Him. It is no more complicated than that. God can completely heal. Nothing is beyond His capabilities, not even mental illness or depression. I surround myself with the things of God. I have immersed myself in the Word of God. The more I read His Word, the closer I feel to Him. I have found that reading the verses about who God says I am, reading the verses about who He is, actually reading them out loud, is a proclaimation of truth over my life. By the power of His Word God created the heavens and the earth, and when I speak His Word His truth brings life to me. I used to say that I was worth nothing and the world would be better off without me. Now, as I speak the truth from the Word of God I remember who I am through the saving grace of Christ. When I can't find words to pray, then I pray the prayers found in Scripture. When I can't find the words to praise, I will speak words of praise from the Psalms. This is how I overcome and find victory in my life.

I have spoken about surrounding myself with the right people. The world is full of people who are happy to sympathise with you. I no longer settle for sympathy. I seek the company of friends who will speak good Biblical principles of truth into my life. If I am honest, these are sometimes harder relationships, but I gain great strength from them because I know that these friends love me enough to challenge me. This makes me a better person.

"As iron sharpens iron, and one person sharpens the wits of another."
(Proverbs 27:17 NRS)

I seek good Godly counsel when decisions need to be made, and I am careful what I put between my ears. I forgive more quickly, seek Him first and talk to Him about everything. I thank Him and worship Him at every opportunity, and I never forget that my hope and my future is in Him. This is what brings victory in my life.

"God doesn't come and go. God lasts. He's Creator of all you can see or imagine. He doesn't get tired out, doesn't pause to catch his breath. And he knows everything, inside and out. He energizes those who get tired, gives fresh strength to dropouts. For even young people tire and drop out, young folk in their prime stumble and fall. But those who wait upon God get fresh strength. They spread their wings and soar like eagles, they run and don't get tired, they walk and don't lag behind."
(Isaiah 40:28-3, The Message)

Depression can affect anyone - male or female, young or old, rich or poor, but those who wait on the Lord will be strengthened. He is my strength and He can be yours. My prayer for you is that you, or someone you love, will also find hope in this testimony.

May God be glorified through these pages.